Diversity Without Divisiveness

Diversity Without Divisiveness: A Guide to DEI Practice for K-12 Educators provides frameworks, touchstones, and tools to help you move beyond the buzzwords and truly practice DEI by fostering a shared vision for inclusive education.

Written by two educators with rich backgrounds in DEI practice and training, this book shows how to promote inclusivity without falling into partisan promotion of prescribed beliefs. Hoyt and Ham address common misunderstandings, explain the crucial interaction between DEI and SEL, and provide language for addressing parents' concerns about DEI. The authors also invite educators to tackle DEI challenges in K–12 education: Should students be assigned to "affinity groups"? How can DEI be integrated into curricula? What are some tools for DEI professional development? How can we mitigate objections from those feeling threatened by inclusivity.

The book offers a plethora of tools to ensure that DEI is not just an ideal to strive for but a tangible reality within every classroom. There are also firsthand accounts from educators who are actively engaging with DEI in impactful ways. With Hoyt and Ham's tangible solutions, you'll be able to chart a course for a more inclusive and equitable school.

Carlos Hoyt, PhD, LICSW, provides consultation, training, and support on matters related to social identity, social bias, and social justice to people and places wishing to create inclusive environments, and psychotherapy for children, adults, couples, and families. Carlos's first book, *The Arc of a Bad Idea: Understanding and Transcending Race*, was published in 2016. He has numerous published works, has presented a TEDx Talk, and appeared on several podcasts. More about Carlos can be found at carloshoyt.com.

Minna Ham, M.S.Ed, works as a lower school director at an independent school in Rhode Island and has been in elementary education and administration for over 20 years. She has presented at conferences and consulted with schools throughout New England on diversity, equity, and inclusivity topics.

Also Available from Routledge
Eye On Education
(www.routledge.com/k-12)

Let's Get Real, 2e:
Exploring Race, Class, and Gender Identities in the Classroom
Martha Caldwell and Oman Frame

Facilitating Conversations about Race in the Classroom
Danielle Stewart, Martha Caldwell, and Dietra Hawkins

Gender and Sexuality in the Classroom:
An Educator's Guide
Marni Brown, Baker A. Rogers, and Martha Caldwell

Identity Affirming Classrooms:
Spaces that Center Humanity
Erica Buchanan-Rivera

Diversity Without Divisiveness

A Guide to DEI Practice
for K-12 Educators

Carlos Hoyt with Minna Ham

NEW YORK AND LONDON

Designed cover image: Concept by Lauren Hoyt

First published 2025
by Routledge
605 Third Avenue, New York, NY 10158

and by Routledge
4 Park Square, Milton Park, Abingdon, Oxon, OX14 4RN

Routledge is an imprint of the Taylor & Francis Group, an informa business

© 2025 Carlos Hoyt and Minna Ham

The right of Carlos Hoyt and Minna Ham to be identified as authors of this work has been asserted in accordance with sections 77 and 78 of the Copyright, Designs and Patents Act 1988.

All rights reserved. The purchase of this copyright material confers the right on the purchasing institution to photocopy or download pages which bear the copyright line at the bottom of the page. No other parts of this book may be reprinted or reproduced or utilised in any form or by any electronic, mechanical, or other means, now known or hereafter invented, including photocopying and recording, or in any information storage or retrieval system, without permission in writing from the publishers.

Trademark notice: Product or corporate names may be trademarks or registered trademarks, and are used only for identification and explanation without intent to infringe.

ISBN: 978-1-032-83982-0 (hbk)
ISBN: 978-1-032-82251-8 (pbk)
ISBN: 978-1-003-51067-3 (ebk)

DOI: 10.4324/9781003510673

Typeset in Palatino
by Apex CoVantage, LLC

Access the Support Material: www.routledge.com/9781032822518

Dedications

Carlos's Dedication

To my mom, Winnifred Hoyt,
Who never needed to read any book
To know how to teach her kids to be
Just, compassionate, honest, humble, and brave

To Don Welch
Revered and beloved teacher, coach, mentor, father, friend
He did not come from where I come from
But he brought me to a place where I could discover where I was going
A place where coming together does not compete with coming from

Minna's Dedication

To Justin Zeller
Our journey together has been a path of growth and transformation
I am forever grateful for the ways we inspire each other to thrive,
laugh, and find joy.

To my parents
You taught me resilience, perseverance, and fortitude
I am who I am because of you

Epigraph

Whoever you are

However you are

You are safe here

Contents

Support Material viii

Preface and Acknowledgments ix

Introduction 1

PART ONE
Misconceptions and Clarifications about DEI in Education 19

1 No One Is Anti-DEI 21

2 A Framework for Diversity Without Divisiveness 36

3 Reconciling Contested Issues Toward Positive Parent-School Partnership 50

4 DEI Integrity 76

PART TWO
Praxis: Touchstones and Tools You Can Use 97

PART THREE
Praxis Pointers: Real-World Applications from Educators in the Field 193

Support Material

The following tools from the book are also available on our website as free downloads, so you can easily print and reproduce them for your own use. To access the materials, go to the book product page at www.routledge.com/9781032822518 (or search for the book title on Routledge.com and click on the book's page), and then click on the link that says Support Material.

- The Social Identity Prism
- The Cauldron of Social Bias
- The DEI Ally Pacts
- The Empathic Inquiry Method

Preface and Acknowledgments

Who Are These People?

Our faces are here together for you to see for several reasons.

While we wish appearance did not matter, we know that it does. We acknowledge the very high likelihood that you're wondering, *Who are these people?*, and we know that for good or ill, your assumptions (inevitable assumptions) will be informed by how we look. We invite you to see not only how we look but also what comes to your mind when you see how we look – because what comes to your mind is what matters.

We hope you might see that we are two people who are happy to be colleagues and friends, humbled and honored to have this amazing opportunity to contribute to the discourse on a crucial area of learning and life. While we each benefit from privilege in some contexts, we are, by dint of our appearances and how too many people have been socialized to register them, adversely racialized humans who bring not only learning, credentials, and expertise to this undertaking but also the daily lifelong lived experience of representing and promoting diversity, fighting for equity, and hoping to be fully included in all the places we are qualified to occupy.

Figure 0.1 Carlos Hoyt and Minna Ham

Education as Facilitation

Education is often referred to as a key to progress and liberation, but if we are to be honest, education is no less the means by which advancement is obstructed and minds are enslaved to oppressive doctrines and destructive codes of conduct. For this reason, teaching must never be just about teaching – teaching the received wisdom, teaching as we were taught, teaching to train or indoctrinate. Teaching must first and foremost be about the transparent purposes of what is being taught, about the honest assessment of how what is taught aligns with its purposes, and about respecting and empowering the learner to carefully choose what to take from what they are taught.

We are often carefully taught things, but the truth is that we are also carelessly, thoughtlessly, osmotically taught things, and both methods can result in a positive or negative result. We are magical, voracious learning machines. But we are vulnerable to soaking up bad information, ingesting pretzel-shaped logics, and developing a taste for prejudices, stereotypes, bigotry, and dogma, each and all of which can become hard to resist – hard even to notice.

This is why we are proud and humbled to be educators; not because we believe we are automatically in the right whenever we are designing a lesson or engaging with learners, but because we understand that education can harm as much as it can help. We take seriously our obligation to respect learners' right to know the *whys* behind the *whats* of teaching, and to support their agency in discerning what is worth learning and what is not.

We believe education is best practiced when it takes the form of facilitation. In the context of education, facilitation is the art and practice of guiding learners on their journey of learning and discovery. It is not about dictating or imparting knowledge in a one-directional flow, but rather about creating an environment where learners can critically engage with ideas, ponder diverse perspectives, and actively participate in the construction of their own understanding. As an educator, to facilitate means to be a curator of possibilities, a catalyst for inquiry, and a supporter of the learner's autonomy in navigating the vast seas of knowledge. The facilitator's role is pivotal in empowering students to synthesize information thoughtfully and discerningly, fostering a lifelong passion for learning, a resilient pursuit of wisdom, and a commitment to translating what is learned into civil, constructive conduct.

At this moment in the evolution of the discourse and practice of diversity, equity, and inclusivity in which questions, skepticism, objection, and cynicism conspire to distort the purpose and proper understanding of DEI, we are honored to offer insights, touchstones, and tools to help educators, students, and parents achieve diversity without divisiveness.

Our Paths Toward a Passion for DEI Done Well

Carlos

I was born in Puerto Limon, Costa Rica, in 1960. I was the second of three kids born to Winnifred and Carlos Hoyt. My elder sister, Sandra, was born in Costa Rica about two years before me, and my younger brother, Kevin, was born in the United States in 1966.

My family came to America in two stages. My mother left Costa Rica in 1963 to come to Boston and work as a maid for families in Boston's affluent suburbs. This meant she was leaving her husband and two young children behind. After working for over a year, my mother was able to save enough money to pay for my sister, my father, and me to come to the United States. We settled in the urban Boston neighborhood of Dorchester, where I was a student in the Boston Public School System (BPS) until seventh grade. While growing up and going to school in Dorchester, my mom worked tirelessly as a maid and as a mom, and my dad worked as tirelessly driving cabs, doing custodial work, and eventually becoming a union carpenter. Over those years we experienced Dorchester's demographics shift from virtually completely white-racialized people to virtually completely black-identified people. Over those years my parents achieved their goals of securing steady employment and sufficient income to overcome the poverty they experienced in Costa Rica, the public assistance they required upon arriving in America, and the prospect of being renters forever. Eventually, they were able to purchase a three-story flat and create a safe, stable, and happy home for the family.

Dissatisfied with the quality of education my sister and I were receiving in BPS, my folks sought better educational settings for both of us. My sister was fortunate to land in a small private school where she found great teachers, great friends, and got a great education. I was accepted into the voluntary school desegregation busing program referred to as METCO (the Metropolitan Council on Economic Opportunity). METCO worked with willing suburban towns to provide transportation and support to black- and Hispanic-identified students willing to go to go far from home and far from the familiar to gain a better education. Our younger brother, Kevin, who faced learning challenges associated with aphasia and autism, received the same level of care and advocacy from my parents as did my sister and I. My folks were successful in facilitating his enrollment in a school that specialized in teaching and nurturing children who needed and deserved educational approaches that were tailored to their particular circumstances.

In my teen years and beyond, I occasionally wrote letters to my parents to try to express my inexpressible gratitude for the depthless love, devotion, and sacrifice they demonstrated. I was surprised when my mother wrote back to me once. Neither she nor my dad were given the opportunity to go to school with regularity or to any degree of completion in Costa Rica or in America. Nevertheless, they were able to gain a sufficient grasp of the language to get by. Here is the note my mother wrote to me:

Dear Jr.,

When we decided to travel to the USA, our main goal was to provide a better life for you; to be able to give you most of the things that we never had, mainly a good education.

Seeing you and your sister and brother through school has been one of our greatest achievements. Nothing more could have been more satisfying.

But we will not take all the credit since we realize that we could not have done it without your cooperation.

Thanks for helping us accomplish our goal.

Now the rest is up to you.

All we ask in return is that you continue to live a productive life full with pride and respect – but above all be happy, since our happiness depends on yours.

We love you and will always be here for you.

Mom

This book, for me, derives from what I have learned about identity, diversity, equity, and inclusion over and across all kinds of contexts and many years – learning that began and was most vivid in the lessons my parents taught through simply living as they did. Costa Rica, Panama, Jamaica, South America, Northern Europe, Scotland, Western Africa, places as yet unknown, and likely never to be known. My relatives and ancestors are from all over this genetically interconnected world (so are yours). My parents faced chronic, painful inequity and exclusion based not on their identities but on the habits of identification and associated treatment of unjust people, systems, structures, and institutions.

My parents demonstrated day in and day out that identity should be about how you choose to move through the world and who you choose to call family. It should not be about parsing the infinite diversity of ways to be human into us and them, in or out, superior and inferior. Family should be about support and sacrifice and service. It should not be about reductive notions of belonging and boundaries of purity and exclusion. To be of service to others, community, and the world is to be successful. To limit one's regard and service to "one's own" is bigotry. Witnessing the exceedingly disproportionate efforts my parents had to make to achieve their modest ambitions made it crystal clear to me that not everyone gets equal or equitable opportunities to pursue life, liberty, and happiness. Everyone should. This book is about helping educators and learners understand how everyone can.

Minna

My parents immigrated to the United States in the 1970s. My mother left South Korea to work as a nurse in New York. There was a nurse shortage in the United States, and many young women from Asian countries came to fill the gaps. My father came to study American history, but soon realized a degree would not materialize into a job. Instead, he opened a women's clothing store in the Bronx. After having my sister and me, my parents moved to a suburban haven on the North Shore of Long Island.

This book represents everything I wish I had learned in school. It embodies everything that I had to learn later in life because lessons, discussions, learning experiences that centered on the explicit teaching about empathy, socialization, racism, etc. did not occur in the classrooms in my nationally ranked public schools. The schools that enabled me to attend an Ivy League college never provided opportunities to explore my identity and my relationship to my peers and to the world. Racialized jokes, comments, and nicknames were ignored, endured and given a pass by adults. Students were left with a gap, an abyss of knowledge and skills that made it difficult for them to navigate a complex and diverse world.

The first people that exposed me to race and racism were my parents. They taught me from a young age that I had to be twice as good to be seen as half as good as people with privileged social status based on their racialization. For good or ill, that has always been in the back of my mind. The sentiment has stuck with me, but so has the idea that it was my parents that gave me my first lesson about racialization. My parents, whose main goal was to keep me safe, saw teaching me about the racialized world as a means of accomplishing this.

As a parent and educator, emphasizing the importance of teaching about the racialized world is crucial. My primary focus lies in dismantling rather than perpetuating its structures. I hope this book will give my parents and others hope that we can move toward a world in which we are not mismeasured and mistreated based on racialization.

Acknowledgments

We extend our profound gratitude to our publisher at Routledge, Lauren Davis, for her confidence in us and our work, and for her ever gracious and responsive oversight and guidance throughout the writing process. We also wish to thank Sean Daly, PhD, Senior Editorial Assistant, Education, and the editorial team who worked diligently with us to refine this work. Heartfelt thanks go to our generous families and friends for their unwavering support, encouragement, and feedback.

We are deeply grateful to our colleagues in education who contributed their applications of work to the Praxis Pointers section of the book. And we are grateful to the many colleagues who, one way or another, helped us develop our thoughts about this undertaking.

Special thanks to Lauren Hoyt for the book cover image, Leslie Hoyt for the photo of Minna and Carlos, and Evan Hoyt for editorial guidance.

This book was developed with the assistance of AI technology, specifically the use of OpenAI's ChatGPT, for research and to inform the technical aspects of writing (grammar, etc.). We clarify that while AI tools were employed for supplementary support functions, all content within this publication is the original work of the authors, reflecting our unique insights, analyses, and creative expressions.

Introduction

Why This Book and Why This Book Right Now

DEI isn't merely a modern-day concept – it's woven into the very fabric of who we are as a socio-diverse species. Determinations about diversity equity, and inclusivity pervade the lives of every human. DEI is at the heart of our nation's founding and its continued aspirations towards a state of liberal democracy and e pluribus unum.

Diversity Without Divisiveness: A Guide to DEI Practice for K-12 Educators unravels the false narrative that DEI is something one should or should not partake in, and, instead, recognizes that DEI is a reality we all participate in, either by expanding its reach or by restricting it. At this markedly contentious moment when it appears that DEI and education are colliding at the intersection of inclusivity and pedagogy, this book invites educators, parents, students, policymakers, leaders and everyone interested in how to get along in increasingly diverse settings to explore, understand, and resolve crucial DEI debates and challenges in K–12 education: Should students be assigned to "affinity groups"? How can DEI be effectively integrated into educational curricula? What should DEI leadership look like? How can we successfully engage with those feeling threatened by DEI practices? Grounded in over six collective decades of expertise, we offer not just insights but tangible solutions to these pressing challenges and chart a course toward more inclusive and equitable schools.

"Touchstones and Tools"

We use the terms "touchstone and tools" to convey the importance of a combination of unifying guiding principles and perspectives for DEI translated into adoptable and adaptable methods of practice. While the term "tools" is likely to have a clear and common meaning for readers, "touchstone" in the context of DEI practice might benefit from explication.

Traditionally, a touchstone is a standard or criterion by which the quality or worth of something is judged. Originally, it referred to a stone used to test the purity of gold and silver by the streak left on the stone when rubbed against it, which allows a comparison to known standards of alloys. In the metaphorical sense, it has come to mean any means of testing worth or genuineness.

In the realm of DEI, a "touchstone" refers to essential principles and foundational truths that serve as benchmarks for evaluating the integrity and efficacy of DEI efforts. These touchstones are not just theoretical concepts but practical, actionable references that guide educators, leaders, and practitioners in ensuring that their DEI initiatives are not only well-intentioned but also anchored in proven strategies and ethical practices.

By returning to these touchstones regularly and checking our work against them, we continuously affirm that our approaches are grounded in a commitment to fairness, inclusivity, and genuine respect for diversity. They help us maintain the integrity of our actions and strategies, ensuring they meet the high standards necessary for efficacious practice. Just as the traditional touchstone was used to test the purity of precious metals, our DEI touchstones allow us to assess the purity and effectiveness of our interventions.

Diversity Without Divisiveness offers several touchstones that we invite readers to consider as they move through the book, and especially as they conduct their DEI pedagogy.

Core DEI Touchstones

DEI-Expansivism: Advocating for equity and inclusivity for the whole wide range of human beings.

Antibias Coalitional Approach: Promoting a unified approach where individuals and groups across different backgrounds come together to combat bias. This coalitional approach emphasizes solidarity and collective action in fostering an equitable society.

Tension Between Private Belief and Public Tolerance: Recognizing and navigating the delicate balance between respecting individual beliefs and maintaining a commitment to public tolerance. This principle underlines the importance of fostering an environment where diverse perspectives coexist respectfully, promoting a collective well-being without compromising personal integrity.

Inclusivity Cannot Be Inclusive of Exclusivity: Upholding the logic premise that true expansivist inclusivity cannot coexist with exclusivity. This touchstone challenges practices and policies that isolate or discriminate, advocating for environments where every individual feels valued and included.

Empathy as a Guiding Principle: Placing empathy at the heart of DEI efforts to understand and address the needs and experiences of all individuals. This involves striving to comprehend others' perspectives and experiences deeply, and fostering communities where empathy drives interactions and decisions.

Understanding Racialization: Educating about racialization as the process by which race and racism are produced. This touchstone encourages the deconstruction of racial categories to address the root causes of racism and dismantle systemic biases.

Continuous Reflection and Adaptation: Emphasizing the need for ongoing self-assessment and responsiveness to change. DEI is viewed as a dynamic field requiring adaptability and continual learning to remain effective and relevant.

Organization of the Book and Overview of Contents

Diversity Without Divisiveness: A Guide to DEI Practice for K-12 Educators is designed to create a *head* to *heart* to *feet* comprehensive treatment of DEI pedagogy and practice that will leave every reader with a clear and unifying understanding of what DEI is (*head*), guidance for how it can be approached constructively and connectively with empathy, self-awareness, humility, and grace (*heart*) through a road-tested collection of methods, and how-to pointers from educators out in the real world utilizing touchstones and tools presented in the book (*feet*). The book is divided into three parts with content as follows.

Part One – Misconceptions and Clarifications about DEI in Education
Part One of *Diversity Without Divisiveness: A Guide to DEI Practice for K-12 Educators* lays the essential groundwork for understanding and embracing the principles of DEI in education. By addressing common misconceptions and presenting a unifying framework, this section prepares educators to lead with an informed and nuanced perspective.

Chapter 1: No One is Anti-DEI – In the first chapter, we clarify what DEI truly encompasses, addressing common misunderstandings and defusing the charged controversies surrounding it. By examining the nuanced realities of DEI, we aim to move beyond buzzwords and establish a foundational understanding for educators.

Chapter 2: A Framework for Diversity Without Divisiveness – This chapter introduces the Social Identity Prism, a comprehensive framework for DEI pedagogy. The Prism is designed to unify educators under a common language and approach, fostering a shared vision for inclusive education. This chapter affirms the crucial interaction between DEI and Social-Emotional Learning (SEL) and DEI and Health & Wellness.

Chapter 3: Reconciling Contested Issues Toward Positive Parent-School Partnership – This chapter delves into the doubts, disagreements, and complaints some parents express about their perception of or experience with DEI practices. Fostering positive parent-school partnerships regarding DEI requires clearly addressing reasonable questions and concerns about DEI.

Chapter 4: DEI Integrity – Chapter 4 provides guidance on DEI leadership, exploring individual, interpersonal, and structural/systemic factors that are crucial to effective and sustainable DEI oversight, and offering strategies for educators to lead with conviction and adaptability in a diverse and sometimes challenging educational landscape.

Together, these chapters provide the context needed for educators to approach DEI not as an added or problematic initiative but as an inextricable aspect of education and an integral part of their teaching philosophy and practice. They set the stage for Part Two, where the theoretical foundation of DEI is translated into practical, actionable strategies that educators can seamlessly integrate into their daily practice. With a firm grasp of DEI's complexities and a shared vision for inclusivity, educators are equipped to foster environments where every student can thrive.

Part Two – Praxis: Touchstones and Tools You Can Use
Part Two of *Diversity Without Divisiveness* is where foundational elements – the touchstones of DEI – are transformed into dynamic instruments of change within educational praxis. This section illustrates the confluence of touchstones and tools, demonstrating how foundational concepts introduced in Part One are operationalized as practical methods in Part Two to create an engaging, inclusive, and equitable learning environment.

For example, the Social Identity Prism introduced as a touchstone in Part One becomes a multifaceted tool in Part Two. It serves as a basis for activities and discussions that delve into the complexities of social identity, social bias, and social justice. By presenting 11 touchstones in Part Two which are operationalized as tools, *Diversity Without Divisiveness* equips educators with a dual-purpose approach to DEI. It encourages them to internalize DEI principles as touchstones of their teaching philosophy and to employ them as tools for fostering a diverse and inclusive educational space. This approach ensures that DEI is not just an ideal to strive for but a tangible reality within every classroom.

In this section, educators will find a curated collection of activities, discussion prompts, case studies, reflective exercises, visuals, policies, communication exemplars, lesson plans, workshop programs, curriculum guidance, and a model to assess belonging. Each tool is designed to be adaptable to various educational settings and student demographics. The goal is to equip educators with the means to implement DEI principles day to day, fostering a learning environment where all students feel valued, understood, and equipped to thrive both academically and personally.

Furthermore, the tools provided in Part Two will support educators in cultivating positive partnerships with parents and guardians by demonstrating the practical benefits of DEI in education. By showcasing how DEI initiatives can enhance the learning experience for all students, educators can build bridges with families and foster a community-wide culture of inclusivity.

Part Three – Praxis Pointers: Real-World Applications from a Community of Practitioners

Part Three, "Praxis Pointers," is the beating heart of *Diversity Without Divisiveness: A Guide to DEI Practice for K-12 Educators*. It's where the content comes alive in the classroom, providing educators with a vibrant tapestry of real-world applications of the DEI principles outlined in previous chapters.

In this section, readers will find a collection of firsthand accounts from educators who have skillfully woven the DEI Touchstones and Tools into the fabric of their teaching environments. Each Praxis Pointer offers a window into the lived experiences of teachers who are actively engaging with DEI in innovative and impactful ways. Each Praxis Pointer will feature the following:

> Information about the Praxis Pointer contributor: A personal introduction to the educators who are making a difference.
> Educational Environments: An explanation of the educational context in which the contributor applied the tool.
> DEI Applications: How the contributor used the tool.
> Methodologies: Concrete narratives of how these tools were applied in practice, offering a step-by-step recount of the educators' approaches.

> Impacts and Outcomes: An honest reflection on the results of these applications, sharing both successes and lessons learned, providing a holistic view of DEI in action.
> Community Connections: Direct contact information for each contributor, fostering a community of collaboration and support that extends beyond the pages of the book.

The Value of "Praxis Pointers

This section leverages the relatability of peer experiences, making the DEI journey accessible and grounded in the real-world challenges and triumphs of fellow educators. Showcasing a spectrum of educational contexts, "Praxis Pointers" illustrates the adaptability of DEI principles across a variety of teaching and community environments. Educators can draw inspiration from detailed examples, using them as blueprints to tailor their DEI efforts to fit their unique circumstances. The inclusion of contact details transforms the book into a springboard for ongoing dialogue and connection, empowering a vibrant network of DEI practitioners.

Establishing a Community of Praxis Pointers Practitioners

Readers of *Diversity Without Divisiveness: A Guide to DEI Practice for K-12 Educators* are invited to not only receive the practicable contributions of others but to contribute their own stories of application of touchstones and tools found in the book, thus co-creating a growing collection of Praxis Pointers through an online exchange platform. QR codes and video links will provide portals into the stories, offering a multimedia dimension to the learning experience and connecting readers with a chorus of voices championing and exemplifying effective DEI. By inviting readers to share their experiences, "Praxis Pointers" becomes a living document, evolving with each new story and strategy shared by educators in the field.

Through "Praxis Pointers," the guide transcends the traditional boundaries of a book to become an interactive, collaborative, diverse, and ever-expanding resource. It's a testament to the power of shared knowledge and the collective commitment of educators to cultivate environments where every student is seen, supported, and celebrated.

Notes on Terminology: A Glossary of Diversity Equity and Inclusivity Crucial Terms and Concepts

Common understanding is the soil of common ground. There's far too good a chance that we don't know what each other is talking about when we talk about many terms and concepts related to diversity, equity, and inclusivity.

How can we constructively talk about "race" and "racism" and "gender" and other important DEI terms constructively when we can't even be sure that we share an understanding of what they mean?

This glossary provides definitions of some key terms in the discourse on *social identity*, *social bias*, and *social justice* (three terms that are closely related to DEI, defined in the glossary). The definitions are grounded in logic (versus mere opinion or tendentious reasoning) and evidence (science). Nevertheless, you might find yourself wanting to add a bit to this one or that one or wanting to apply special emphasis to something about that one or this one. In other words, some of the definitions you'll find here might not strike you as "exact" enough. If so, that's OK. We can hold somewhat different senses of what a word means and still communicate meaningfully. Consider, for example, a conversation about love. People will likely have a general shared understanding of what love is, but it's also likely that there would be disagreement about, for example, when "like" becomes "love" or what constitutes loving behavior. When it comes to DEI terms and concepts, as long we don't lose connection to evidence and logic, and as long as we take the time to compare meanings and come to agreement on what we mean when we are talking about a term or concept, we should be able to talk constructively with one another.

First things first: Why do we use "inclusivity" instead of "inclusion" as the "I" in DEI?

Before providing the glossary, it's important to try to explain why we prefer what might seem like a small semantic shift from "inclusion" to "inclusivity" as the "I" in DEI.

Inclusion is to inclusivity as diverse is to diversity, and as equitable is to equity. In each relationship, the first term denotes an outcome, and the second term denotes the principle or quality that animates the first term. *Inclusion* is the *outcome* of effective practices rooted in a commitment to *inclusivity*, the view that everyone deserves to feel safe, seen, welcome, respected, valued, and represented; a combination of qualities that results in a sense of belonging. Inclusivity is the principle that drives efforts to achieve inclusion. *We recognize the logic and fairness of social enfranchisement for all members of society; therefore, we strive to bring about inclusion for all.*

Equity is the quality of being fair and impartial (the principle), while *equitable* refers to something characterized by equity or fairness (the outcome). *We recognize equity as necessary in achieving equality of opportunity; therefore, we strive to bring about equity for all members of society.*

Diversity is the principle that drives effort to achieve a diverse collection of people (and non-human organisms as well). *Diverse* is the state of being composed of different types; a state of variety (the outcome). *We recognize the power of heterogeneous groups in constructive interaction; therefore, we seek to achieve and/or maintain environments characterized by diverse sets of people (and non-human organisms as well).*

A DEI Glossary (Terms Appear More or Less in the Order of Relation to One Another Versus Alphabetically)

DEI-Expansivism and DEI-Restrictivism: DEI-Expansivism refers to greater and greater inclusion of the total diversity of ways to be human. DEI-Restrictivism refers to limiting the range of acceptable ways to be human, restricting the benefits of equality and equity to only those determined to be in preferred groups, and excluding unfavored groups.

Antibias – resistance and opposition to forces of exclusion, discrimination, or oppression, however they manifest (e.g., as sexism, racism, ableism, lookism, classism, etc.).

An important note about antibias language and "race":

Efforts to be antibias must include avoiding or correcting language that represents, perpetuates, or reinforces false, reductive, essentialist, or oppressive constructions of social identity.

For that reason, this book will not use language commonly used to describe people *as members of races*. Labelling people as members of races abets a highly problematic practice of human categorization that has led to needless and tragic division and harm. It is good that there is growing understanding that race is a social construct and not biological, genetic, scientific reality, but acknowledging that the concept of race is a social construct and then persisting in perpetuating it as a way to categorize, divide, or even unite people is like knowing that the Earth isn't flat and persisting in navigating it as if it were.

Instead of perpetuating the harmful habit of acting as if people can and should be labelled as black or white, the terms, *"black-racialized," "white-racialized," "white-identified,"* or *"black-identified"* will be used. This will likely strike many eyes and ears as clunky and stilted, but that is only because it is unfamiliar and challenges a convention in which most of us are deeply entwined and invested. We can't be effectively antibias unless we are willing to combat not only systemic policies but also the psychologies, worldviews, and habits of mind that keep us attached to harmful practices. Resisting language that reifies and reinforces false and harmful differences is essential to overcoming social bias.

Social Construct: A social construct is an idea or notion that is perceived as natural and obvious to people who accept it but does not represent an inherent aspect of reality (e.g., a set of stars versus the named constellation of the set of stars).

A social construct is an agreed-upon concept that has relevance and impact because people within a society behave as if it exists. It is maintained over time through social consensus and institutions, and often has significant consequences on how society is organized and how individuals interact with each other. Through such reification processes, social constructs become embedded in the fabric of society, acquiring a sense of objectivity and tangibility.

Examples include gender roles, racialization categories, and the notion of money as a medium of exchange. They have no objective basis in nature but are made meaningful within societies. Social constructs can have profound and tangible effects on people's lives, including legal implications, access to resources, and social status.

Common Ground – An area of agreement that allows people to work together positively.

Diversity – when referring to people, diversity typically means people whose identities, characteristics, and backgrounds differ from one another. One person cannot be diverse. Only a group of people can be diverse.

Equity – Equity means providing people with what they need so that they can experience life, liberty, and the pursuit of happiness without having to contend with social bias or other forms of unfair disadvantage.

Inclusivity – Inclusivity means treating all community members in ways that lead them to feel a sense of belonging, equal representation, value, and support – versus mere inclusion, which can stop short of achieving belonging and only result in nominal or token or otherwise insubstantial participation.

"DEI" versus "DEIB" or "DEIJ/JEDI" – Consistent with the overwhelming prevalence of the use of "DEI" to describe matters related to diversity, equity, and inclusivity in academia and the media, and also to practice parsimony in the use of terminology, we use "DEI" in this book and advocate for its use as the standard way to refer to matters related to diversity, equity, and inclusivity. Because "DEIB," where the "B" stands for belonging, and "DEIJ" (or sometimes "JEDI") are used by some people and groups, we provide the following consideration of why belonging and justice do not need explicit reference by way of adding "B" or "J" to DEI.

Inclusivity and Belonging

When inclusivity is effectively implemented, it naturally fosters a sense of belonging. Belonging goes beyond just being allowed to be present; it's the social-emotional outcome that arises from genuine inclusivity. It's the internal sense of being an integral part of a group (not merely a token presence), being accepted for who you are, and feeling safe to express yourself without fear of discrimination or exclusion.

Adding a "B" for belonging to the DEI acronym might suggest that belonging is a separate, standalone concept from inclusivity, which could dilute the focus on the actions and policies necessary to create inclusive environments. Instead, the aim should be to underscore that true inclusivity is the means by which belonging is achieved. In this sense, belonging is the litmus test for inclusivity – without a sense of belonging, inclusivity has not been fully realized.

Equity and Justice

The "E" in DEI, which stands for equity, is intrinsically connected to the concept of justice. Equity is the practice of allocating resources, opportunities, and treatment based on the unique needs and circumstances of individuals or groups. It's about fairness in the process of providing what is needed for people to experience life, liberty, and the pursuit of happiness without unfair burdens of bias and discrimination.

Justice is a construct that can vary significantly based on the social system in which it is applied. Each society defines justice through its laws, norms, values, and cultural understandings. These definitions are often enshrined in a legal framework that outlines the rights and wrongs and the rewards and punishments, that apply to members of the community. Determining whether something is just involves measuring actions, policies, and outcomes against these established definitions within the given social system. A just act in one cultural context may be perceived differently in another based on varying societal laws and moral philosophies.

Equity, on the other hand, is concerned with fairness in terms of needs and opportunities. It is about tailoring the distribution of resources, support, and access so that individuals can achieve an equal shot at success (broadly and variably defined). To assess equity, we look at individual circumstances and structural factors that impact people's lives. We then ask if the measures in place are sufficient to address imbalances and meet diverse needs. Equity requires ongoing evaluation and adjustment, as the needs of individuals and communities can change over time.

The relationship between justice and equity is dynamic. A society's conception of justice informs what is considered equitable within that context. At the same time, striving for equity can lead to a re-examination of what is considered just, potentially transforming laws and societal norms.

In essence, justice provides the rules of the game, while equity ensures that everyone has an adequate opportunity to play, regardless of their starting point. For everyone to truly be treated the same under the law (justice), there must be a recognition that we do not all start from the same place or live in the same circumstances due to historical and structural inequalities. Equity is the about making adjustments to address these imbalances.

Adding a "J" for justice to the DEI acronym might suggest that justice is somehow separate from equity. However, equity is critical to addressing disparities and achieving justice in diverse societies. To separate justice and treat it as an additive concept to DEI is to misunderstand the integral role equity plays in achieving just outcomes. Therefore, there is no need to add a "J" for justice to DEI, because a commitment to equity is already a commitment to justice; though not identical, the two are inseparable in aim and function. Through the pursuit of equity, we are actively engaging in the work of justice – striving to right imbalances and create a society where every individual has the opportunity to succeed without unfair barriers.

Social Identity – Every society defines identity categories that are important in understanding who people are and that often act as the basis for how people are treated. Typical social identity categories include *Family-Ethnicity-Heritage, Physical Appearance, Age, Ability, Gender, Race, Sexual Orientation, Social Status, and Worldview-Belief System.* Your social identity is how others see you in terms of these categories. Often how society sees or defines you matches how you see and define yourself, but not always. For example, a person might be seen and categorized by others as one gender while thinking of themselves in a different way regarding gender.

Social Bias – "Bias" means "leaning." For a physical example, think of the Leaning Tower of Pisa. It leans in a certain direction (and away from the opposite direction). Social bias is leaning towards or away from a person or people because they are categorized as members of a social identity group. Social bias takes the form of privileging some social identity groups (for example male-identified people, white-identified people, and people with wealth) and discriminating against other social identity groups (for example, black-identified, indigenous-identified, Hispanic-Latino-identified, female-identified, trans-identified, and other marginalized groups).

Social Justice – *Equity*, which means providing what individuals and groups need in order to have equal opportunity, security, health, education, and other social necessities, is at the heart of social justice. Achieving social justice is not about treating everyone equally. For example, some people need and deserve wheelchairs, ramps, and elevators in order to enter and move around buildings. It wouldn't make sense to say that if some people have wheelchairs, then everyone must have a wheelchair in order to achieve equality. Based on things like age, ability, social status, and other factors, different people will always need different things to be fully and fairly included in society.

Socialization – The processes, explicit and implicit, by which individuals acquire worldviews, beliefs, values, and codes of conduct that align with and reflect the norms of the groups in which they are socialized.

Social Identity Supremacy – The belief that people categorized as members of a particular social identity group are superior to those categorized as members of other social identity groups, and that they are therefore entitled to more power, privileges, and social goods of all kinds.

Unearned Privilege/Social Advantage – Power, status, protection, opportunity, and benefits provided to individuals and groups based on the false belief that they are superior and entitled to be treated better than others.

Social Disadvantage – The unwarranted deprivation of power, status, protection, and benefits for individuals and groups at interpersonal, intergroup, structural, systemic, or institutional levels.

Oppression – To exercise power interpersonally, structurally, systemically, or institutionally over others in ways that deny their dignity, freedom, or rights to just treatment.

Essentialize – To infer or determine a set of qualities something must have in order to be what it is. For example, having two hydrogen and one oxygen molecules is essential to being water. When applied to people, essentialism is believing and acting as if kinds/groups of people have inherent (natural), fixed identity-defining characteristics. This might play out in someone thinking, for example, that it is in the nature of people perceived to be members of such and such a social identity group to believe and act in certain ways that are unavoidably and inescapably natural to them. Below are two examples of how essentialism shows up in social identity categorization.

Gender Essentialism – This might manifest in the belief that all women are naturally more nurturing and better caregivers than men. This type of essentialism can lead to discriminatory hiring practices such as preferring women for nursing or teaching roles based on the assumption that these 'caring' qualities are inherent to all women.

Racial Essentialism – An example would be the assumption that all individuals of a certain race share the same intelligence level or athletic ability. For instance, saying that all people of Asian descent are inherently good at mathematics or that all African Americans are naturally athletic perpetuates harmful stereotypes and overlooks the individual abilities and interests of each person.

Family-Ethnicity-Heritage – Your family composition; where you and your relatives come from; the languages you and your relatives speak; the values and culture associated with your background.

Physical Appearance – How you look; your body shape and features (skin color, hair type and color, eye color, height, weight, etc.); the way you dress, etc.

Age – How old you are in actual age (chronological) and as a stage of maturity (e.g., infant, toddler, child, teen, young adult, adult, senior citizen).

Ability – How you are able to do something that matters in society (e.g., sight, hearing, academics, athletics, etc.).

Sex – In many cultures/societies, sex is assigned at birth based on a combination of internal biology (e.g., chromosomes and hormones), and reproductive anatomy (e.g., a uterus), and external anatomy (i.e., visible genitalia). Based on these indicators, medical professionals are authorized to place people into male, female, or intersex categories. Babies with a vulva and no penis are assigned to the female sex category. Babies with a penis and no vulva are assigned to the male sex category. When physically visible indicators are ambiguous, sometimes medical professionals perform surgical alterations to a newborn's genitalia to make them more clearly match what is commonly associated with male or female external anatomy.

Personal Gender identity – How each individual defines their gender. It is an internal feeling or sense a person has of being male, female, both, neither, somewhere in between, or something else altogether. Sometimes people's gender identity matches the sex they were assigned at birth and sometimes it does not. A person may be born with a penis and identify as a boy or born with a vagina and identify as a girl. These people have a gender identity that is called "cisgender" ("cis" meaning *on the same side of* or *matching with*). Or someone may be born with a penis and identify as a girl or be born with a vagina and identify as a boy. These people may have a gender identity called "transgender" ("trans" meaning *across from* or *not matching*). The way a person sees themselves may not fit into female-male categories. This might be referred to as "gender expansive," "genderqueer," "gender nonbinary," or something else. Some people may not want to use a gender label to describe themselves.

Social Gender – Social gender is how a given society defines and constructs gender, assigns people to gender categories, and the expectations it places on people to conform to those definitions, roles, and norms.

Gender Expression – Gender expression is how a person chooses to present any aspect of their gender identity – through physical appearance, apparel, behaviors, pronouns, name, etc. Gender expression may or may not correspond with societal constructions and expectations.

Sexual Orientation – The types of people a person is sexually attracted to. Sexual orientations include heterosexual (male-female), homosexual (sexual attraction to people whose sex is the same as yours – male-male or female-female), bisexual (sexual attraction to people whose sex is the same or opposite), asexual (feeling no sexual attraction to other people), pansexual (feeling sexual attraction to people regardless of their sex), being unsure about your sexual attraction, or other orientations than the ones stated here.

Racialization – Racialization is the process by which a single human mind, a community of human minds, or an entire society creates the concept and construct of race and the associated ideology, doctrine, and practice of racism. It involves five simple steps:

1. *Selecting* some human characteristics as meaningful signs of human difference
2. *Sorting* people into subpopulations based on selected distinctions
3. *Attributing* traits (temperament, talents, behaviors, etc.) to the subpopulations
4. *Essentializing* the differences – conceiving of them as natural, immutable, and hereditary
5. *Acting* as if the differences justify unequal treatment

Race – Socially created (imagined by human minds), scientifically false (lacking evidence) categories of human differences based on vague and variable mixes of appearance and ancestry produced by the process of racialization.

Social Status – The stature, standing, or power a person has based on their wealth, education, access to powerful people, etc.

Worldview-Belief System – The lenses through which a person views and makes sense of how the world is and should be.

"+" – The "+" symbol in the Social Identity Prism is meant to acknowledge any other social identity or identities important to a person but not represented or well enough represented in a system of social identity categorization.

Racism – Regarding people, in thought or deed, as if they can and should be divided into racial categories and treated differently accordingly. Racism is a product of the process of racialization.

Structural, Systemic, and Institutional Bias – Structural bias refers to inequities embedded in the social arrangements that govern human interaction. For example, students and families are differentially impacted by the start and end times of a school day depending on how far from school they live, what the employment schedules and demands on the parents are, etc. Systemic bias refers to the procedures and practices that can have both intended and unintended consequences. For example, a school's grading system, while applied equally to all students, might disadvantage students who deserve accommodation that might not be in place. Institutional bias refers to structures and practices embraced by a given organization which, though they may represent tradition and custom, might also result in advantaging some while disadvantaging others. For example, legacy preference in admissions practices favor those whose families have the benefit of generational attendance and disadvantage those who don't.

Intersectionality – Refers to the many ways that power, privilege, and oppression impact people differently depending on the social identities they are perceived to represent. For example, a person who is black-identified and female will likely experience sexism differently than a person who is white-identified and female. Although "intersectionality" has become the commonly used term for this important dynamic, "confluence" may be a more accurate and useful way to understand that our various and variable social identities are not in geometric relation to one another but instead in fluid interaction.

Empathy – Understanding how another person feels without necessarily feeling what they feel or approving of it. Empathy is not sympathy, compassion, or pity; it is the act of using one's imagination to apprehend what another person is feeling.

Prejudice –Technically, prejudice is simply a disposition towards something or a person or group that is not necessarily based on actual experience with the thing or people. In common usage, the term typically connotes negative constructions of people or groups without reasonable basis.

Stereotype – "Stereotype" comes from the term for creating templates for printing that can be used over and over without variation. This idea, when applied to understanding human beings, refers to casting people with unique qualities into a sameness that can be reductive, offensive, and harmful.

Implicit Bias – Prejudices we are unaware of that might lead us to favor or discriminate against people based on their perceived membership in a particular social identity group.

Microaggression – Small unintended actions towards people based on stereotypes, prejudices, or implicit biases that result in offense and/or degradation. "Microaggression" is perhaps best understood as a term that connotes *social identity indignities*. They might not actually stem from "aggressive" behavior but instead from ignorance or even positive intent – which, of course, does not mitigate against their negative impact.

Allyship – Treating the challenges of people assigned to different social identity groups than yours as if they were your own and providing your support accordingly.

Power – The capacity to direct, determine, or influence the conditions or conduct of oneself or others. In the context of DEI, power is the capacity to shape societal norms, structures, and practices that advance diversity, equity, and inclusivity in expansivist or restrictivist ways. People, structures, systems, and institutions exert their power (through policy-making, cultural narratives, and social interactions) to define the parameters of what counts as a legitimate, acceptable range of human diversity (e.g., are non-binary gender orientations recognized as within or outside the natural range of gender diversity, or is the range restricted to male and female?), who is treated equally and equitably and who is relegated to inferior statuses unworthy of equal and equitable treatment, and whose sense of belonging (fostered through welcoming and valuing their presence, voice, and participation) is considered important.

Reflection and Praxis Prompts

Reflection Prompts

1. Reflect on your initial thoughts when you encounter the terms "diversity," "equity," and "inclusivity." What sources or experiences inform your thoughts about DEI? How do they align or differ from the perspective presented in the introduction?
2. Consider a time when DEI felt like a divisive topic within your educational environment. How might the approach outlined in the introduction have changed that dynamic?
3. What does the phrase "DEI is woven into the very fabric of who we are as a socio-diverse species" mean to you? Can you think of examples from your personal or professional life that illustrate this idea?

4. How does the introduction's portrayal of DEI challenge or reinforce your understanding of the role of educators in fostering inclusive classrooms?
5. In what ways can understanding DEI as a reality we all participate in change the conversation about inclusivity in your school or community?

Praxis Prompts
1. In collaboration with your students, draft a "DEI Vision Statement" for your classroom or school that encapsulates the integrated approach to DEI suggested in the introduction.
2. Identify one aspect of your current educational practice that could be enhanced by the DEI principles outlined in the introduction. Create a plan to implement this change.
3. Assemble a focus group comprising educators, parents, and students to discuss and explore the DEI debates highlighted in the introduction. Use the feedback to inform a practical DEI strategy for your setting.

PART ONE

Misconceptions and Clarifications about DEI in Education

PART ONE

1

No One Is Anti-DEI

Chapter 1 Quick Capture

Diversity, equity, and inclusivity (DEI) represent a trio of fundamental elements of human interaction. *Diversity* encompasses the infinite variety of ways to be human; *equity* seeks to ensure fairness in treatment and opportunities; and *inclusivity* is about efforts to make sure that community members feel safe, valued, respected, and represented.

DEI is as elemental to human life as H_2O, the chemical basis of water. Everyone interacts with water in many ways, including trying to manage it in ways that meet their needs and realize their visions. This is true for diversity, equity, and inclusivity as well.

Asking whether or not DEI per se is a good or a bad thing that people should or should not support is like asking if water is a good or bad thing. The crucial question is, *do we approach DEI expansively or restrictively?*

This understanding invites an open dialogue on the various ways DEI can manifest, without preordaining a singular outcome. This corrective reframing encourages a shared acknowledgment of DEI's elemental importance in human life while inviting diverse viewpoints on how best to manage it.

Introduction

A Google search of the term "anti-DEI" returned 408,000,000 results on the day we sent this manuscript to the publisher. The fact that usage of the term "anti-DEI" and the propagation of a pro-DEI versus anti-DEI conflict are so prevalent could quite understandably lead one to think that there must be substance to the claim that DEI is something that some people support and other people oppose. But the fact that a falsehood is common is not the same as a falsehood being fact.

Any book about diversity, equity, and inclusivity should provide a clear understanding of what DEI is and what it is not. Especially in light of recent efforts to frame DEI as a divisive issue, it's crucial to be clear at the outset of this book that DEI is not something that anyone can be against. No one can be anti-DEI because DEI is essential to humanity. To be human is to automatically participate in the dynamics of diversity, equity, and inclusivity every day and throughout one's lifetime of interactions with other human beings. To understand why this is so, let's refine our understanding of what DEI is.

DEI Is as Elemental as H_2O

The Cambridge Dictionary defines DEI as

> [T]he abbreviation for diversity, equity and inclusion: the idea that all people should have equal rights and treatment and be welcomed and included, so that they do not experience any disadvantage because of belonging to a particular group, and that each person should be given the same opportunities as others according to their needs.[1]

This definition is a bit problematic in that it conflates the dynamic interaction of three essential characteristics of human interaction with a prescribed outcome of their interaction. This is part of the reason there is resistance on the part of some who rail against what they believe DEI to be about. The distinction between *the fundamental components of DEI* and the preferred outcomes of their interaction is crucial for fostering an accurate and nuanced understanding and dialogue around DEI.

By way of analogy, the Cambridge Dictionary provides this definition of H_2O: "*the chemical symbol for water; used to refer to the substance water: H_2O means that each water molecule contains one oxygen and two hydrogen atoms.*"[2] It explains what each component of the abbreviation means and how they interact to produce something we call water. It does *not* prescribe any specific form that water should take (e.g., always boiling, always frozen, always salty, etc.). Water can take many forms.

H_2O stands for water – something that no one can nor should try to dispute. What people can and must determine for themselves is what should be done with water, how they should interact with water, how water management should play out, etc. If we correct our understanding of DEI in this way, we create a common ground of basic understanding that no one could or should try to dispute, a common ground on which candid and constructive discussion and debate about how to approach DEI can take place. This chapter explains and explores the two basic views on how DEI should play out: one being in a *DEI-expansivist* direction. A DEI-expansivist approach is represented in the Cambridge Dictionary definition:

> [T]he idea that all people should have equal rights and treatment and be welcomed and included, so that they do not experience any disadvantage because of belonging to a particular group, and that each person should be given the same opportunities as others according to their needs.[3]

The other way that DEI can play out is in a *DEI-restrictivist* direction, represented by those who object to expanding rights and opportunities to social identity groups they feel should not be granted equal or equitable treatment.

DEI, much like H_2O, can be understood as a combination of essential elements that interact in dynamic ways to shape human experiences and societal structures. *Diversity* refers to the range of human differences, including but not limited to family-ethnicity-heritage, age, physical appearance, ability, gender, sexual orientation, racialization, social status, and worldview/ideology. *Equity* involves ensuring fair treatment and equality of opportunity (though not equality of outcome) by actively working to identify and eliminate barriers that prevent the full participation of some groups. *Inclusivity* is the practice of creating environments in which any individual or group can feel a sense of belonging, safety, welcome, respect, and support.

Understanding DEI in this way – as an essential molecular aspect of the human condition rather than a prescriptive outcome – opens up space for more constructive discussions on how these principles can be applied and operationalized within various contexts. It acknowledges that while the components of DEI are universal, how they are approached and treated depends on the perspectives and purposes of actors at individual, group, institutional, and governmental levels.

We're All DEI Practitioners

To the extent that you have choices about which other humans you spend time with, you are making diversity determinations. As soon as you are interacting with other humans, you are unavoidably treating each and all of them with some degree or another of equity and inclusivity. You are a DEI-agentic organism; therefore, it makes no sense to say that you (or anyone else) are against DEI. To be against DEI would be tantamount to being against interacting with any other humans – which itself would be a diversity stance, an extremely DEI-restrictive one but a DEI stance nonetheless.

> Are you ever in the company of at least one other human being?
> Do you have your druthers regarding who you'd like to spend time with?
> Do you engage with other human beings with a sense of how they should be treated?
> Of course, of course, and of course. Of course, you are a DEI practitioner. Everyone is.

Who will come to your gathering? Whose gathering will you attend? Will seats be assigned at the dinner party, or will everyone be allowed to sit wherever they please? Will you make special accommodations for the older guests or arrange a kids' table? Will vegetarian dishes be included? Will folks be asked to notify you about food allergies? If some folks are traveling from far away to get to your gathering, will you arrange lodging for them close to your home, or maybe even in your home?

These are all DEI questions that lead to DEI answers and actions. What distinguishes some people from others is how they answer DEI questions.

There Are Two Kinds of DEI Practitioners in This World

A clever article that appeared in the *New York Times* in January 2021 was titled and described as follows. "Let's Become More Divided – In this time of hyperpartisanship, leave it to writers to put us all into pens."[4] The article is a collection of drawings and captions that depict humorous binaries and dualities, such as

> There are two kinds of people in this world: those who know where their high school yearbook is and those who do not.
> – Sloane Crosley, "I Was Told There'd Be Cake"

> For me, all people are divided into two groups – those who laugh, and those who smile.
> – Vladimir Nabokov, "Think, Write, Speak"

> Freddie, there are two kinds of people in this world, and you ain't one of them.
> – Dolly Parton, in "Rhinestone"

When it comes to DEI, it's not that there are two kinds of people in this world; one who is in favor of DEI and one who is not. It's that there are two kinds of DEI people, those who are *DEI-expansivist* and those who are *DEI-restrictivist*. The question is not whether you are for or against DEI, it's: What kind of DEI do you advocate?

An *expansivist* approach to DEI embraces the broadening of opportunities and rights to ever more diverse groups of people. This approach aligns with the principles outlined in the Declaration of Independence, promising that "all men are created equal." Expansivist moments in American history include the abolition of slavery, the women's suffrage movement, the Civil Rights Movement, and the LGBTQ+ rights movement. In each of these moments, the nation moved towards more inclusive definitions of who deserves the full benefits and protections of citizenship.

On the other hand, a *restrictivist* approach to DEI is characterized by efforts to limit the extension of rights, opportunities, and inclusivity to certain groups. This approach may be fueled by fear, prejudice, or the desire to maintain existing power structures. Restrictivist moments include the Indian Removal Act, the Chinese Exclusion Act, Jim Crow laws, Japanese internment during World War II, and more recent debates over immigration, voting rights, and legislation against gender inclusivity and teaching about race and racism.

If you read or hear about DEI in and of itself as something that is in dispute, remember that that is a nonsensical thing to think or declare. Similarly, if you hear someone denounce DEI as a bad thing per se, please realize that that also makes no sense. Dismissing or deriding DEI is like saying that being human is bad. We can certainly debate about better and worse ways to be human, and there are certainly better and worse ways to practice DEI, but it makes no sense to generalize or totalize about DEI – negatively or positively.

DEI Is in Our DNA

From the earliest gatherings around ancient fires to the complex, globalized society of today, questions of diversity, equity, and inclusivity have been a constitutive element of the human journey. If you are human, you are a member of a *socio-diverse* species – we are social and we are diverse. Being

Homo sapiens socialis, we might say, we navigate a world rich in diversity, making decisions about inclusivity and fairness at every turn. *What are the types, and what is the range of ways to be human that we consider acceptable? What are our expectations for conformity with this or that way of being human? How do we determine what different kinds of humans deserve in terms of security, opportunity, representation, and privileges?* These questions are not mere abstractions; they are the lived dynamic realities that have shaped our social fabric since time immemorial. DEI is not a modern invention but a timeless aspect of our humanity, embedded in our interactions, our communities, and our collective consciousness.

Furthermore, DEI is in our DNA in the most literal and expansive senses. Biologically, our survival as a species has been shaped by natural selection, a process that thrives on diversity and determines what forms of life will be present and how each will express itself within the survival-defining parameters of any given environment. The genetic variation among individuals and populations is the raw material for evolution, enabling us to adapt to changing environments and challenges. It is our biological diversity that has allowed us to thrive in habitats across the globe.

Just as biodiversity is critical to the resilience and adaptability of ecosystems, so too is socio-diversity, equity, and inclusivity critical to the resilience and adaptability of human communities. In this sense, DEI is not just a moral or social ideal but a fundamental principle that underpins the flourishing and survival of our species in a deeply interconnected world.

DEI Is as American as Apple Pie

Some people, including powerful and high-profile figures and leaders in government and the media, cast DEI as bad for America and inconsistent with what it means to be American. It's important to see past this rhetoric and recognize the irony that the founding and aspirations of America are inextricably rooted in DEI. Here is some evidence of this truth.

1. Founding Principles

The United States was established on principles that highlight the values of equality and freedom, as articulated in founding documents such as the Declaration of Independence: "We hold these truths to be self-evident, that all men are created equal . . ." While the nation's history includes deep and painful contradictions of these principles (e.g., slavery, disenfranchisement of women, and the dispossession of Native Americans), the aspirations and principles themselves are deeply aligned with expansive DEI.

2. A Nation of Immigrants

From its earliest days, the United States has been a diverse nation, described often as a "melting pot" or a "nation of immigrants." The very fabric of the country is woven from the threads of diverse cultures, ethnicities, and traditions. Rejecting DEI is akin to rejecting this fundamental aspect of the American identity.

3. Democratic Ideals

Central to American democracy is the belief in equal representation and equal protection under the law. DEI principles are entirely consistent with this, as they advocate for fair treatment and equal opportunity for all, irrespective of their background. Arguments that position DEI as anti-American can in and of themselves be viewed as anti-American and anti-democratic in that they oppose these foundational aspirations for equal representation and justice for all.

4. First Amendment and Pluralism

The First Amendment to the United States Constitution protects freedoms concerning religion (including non-religious beliefs), expression, assembly, and the right to petition. It guarantees the freedom for a plurality of voices and beliefs to coexist – a core tenet of a diverse and inclusive society. Arguments against DEI could be seen as contrary to this essential American commitment to pluralism and free expression.

5. The Pursuit of a 'More Perfect Union'

The preamble to the U.S. Constitution begins with the aim to "form a more perfect Union." This implies a continual process of improvement and growth. DEI is an inherent and essential part of this evolution – efforts to make the country more just, more equal, and more inclusive, which is in line with the Constitution's vision. Those who argue that DEI is anti-American are resisting this foundational aspiration for progress and betterment toward maximal inclusivity.

The term "American experiment" is often used to refer to the unique democratic endeavor started by the Founding Fathers of the United States. It speaks to the idea that America, as a democratic republic built on the principles of individual freedom and equality, was a novel and experimental venture in governance at the time of its establishment. This experiment involved breaking away from the long-established monarchies and rigid social hierarchies of Europe to form a nation where power stemmed from the people and individual rights were protected. As such, the very motivation to found this country and commence "the American experiment" was essentially about diversity, equity, and inclusivity – and the nation has been reckoning with what that should mean ever since.

To put this specifically in terms of DEI, first consider the diversity of the early settlers. They were a collection of people from various parts of Europe, each bringing different cultural backgrounds, religions, and worldviews. This diversity was seen as a strength that fueled innovation, cultural exchange, and the creation of a society distinct from the rigid structures of Europe.

Second, the idea of equity is inherent in the founding principles of the United States, as outlined in the Declaration of Independence: "We hold these truths to be self-evident, that all men are created equal, that they are endowed by their Creator with certain unalienable Rights, that among these are Life, Liberty and the pursuit of Happiness." These words reflect a fundamental commitment to the notion that every individual should have an equal opportunity to succeed and thrive – notwithstanding the obvious exclusion of non-white-identified males in the original language of the Declaration.

Third, inclusivity is reflected in the concept of e pluribus unum – "out of many, one." This Latin motto, found on the Great Seal of the United States, expresses the vision of uniting people from many backgrounds into a single nation.

Of course, the reality of American history is complex, and our aspirational reach has woefully and tragically exceeded our grasp on too many occasions. The founders themselves, despite espousing principles of equality and liberty, maintained institutions of slavery and denied the rights of indigenous peoples, women, and others who were not white-racialized, male landowners. Furthermore, religious, ethnic, and racial intolerance has been a recurrent issue throughout the nation's history.

The American experiment has, from the outset, been an ongoing endeavor to establish "the most perfect union" of diversity, equity, and inclusivity. The ideals were there at the beginning, but the realization of these ideals has been a long and continuous struggle – a struggle that continues today. From the Civil Rights Movement to the ongoing fight for gender equality, LGBTQ+ rights, disability rights, and the rights of immigrants and religious minorities, the United States is continually evolving its understanding of what diversity, equity, and inclusivity truly mean.

A Brief History of DEI Initiatives and Milestones

The concept of diversity, equity, and inclusivity (DEI) has roots that can be traced back to the beginning of human history. Throughout human history, human interactions have been characterized by individuals needing to find ways to work out differences, whether through cooperation, compromise, or conflict. Diversity, in terms of the differences among people, has always been a natural and inescapable aspect of the human condition.

One of the primordial aspects of the human condition is the diversity of roles and distribution of power and resources. Throughout history, differently organized human groups have needed to reckon with diversity and questions of equity and inclusivity. From families, to tribes, to nations, and from classrooms, to church groups, to corporations, every human group has its history of DEI-expansive or DEI-restrictive actions. Examples of this from the American perspective include the following:

DEI-Expansivist Milestones

1776: The founding of America is essentially about diversity, equity, and inclusivity.

1861–1865: The Civil War in the United States is fought over issues of diversity, equity, and inclusivity.

1920: The Nineteenth Amendment to the United States Constitution is ratified, granting women the right to vote.

1941: President Franklin D. Roosevelt signs Executive Order 8802, which prohibited racial discrimination in the national defense industry.

1948: President Harry S. Truman's Executive Order 9981 desegregates the military.

1954: The Supreme Court case *Brown v. Board of Education* declares that separate educational facilities are inherently unequal.

1957: The Little Rock Nine, a group of African American students, are the first to desegregate Little Rock Central High School in Arkansas.

1960: The Greensboro Four, four African American college students, begin a sit-in at a Woolworth's lunch counter in Greensboro, North Carolina.

1964: The Civil Rights Act of 1964 is passed.

1965: The Voting Rights Act is signed into law.

1967: *Loving v. Virginia*: The Supreme Court strikes down state laws prohibiting "interracial" marriage.

1967: President Lyndon B. Johnson signs Executive Order 11375 prohibiting discrimination in federal employment on the basis of sex.

1968: The Fair Housing Act is passed.

1971: The *Swann v. Charlotte-Mecklenburg Board of Education* Supreme Court case affirms busing.

1972: Title IX of the Education Amendments is passed, barring exclusion from participation in educational programs based on sex.

1975: The Individuals with Disabilities Education Act (IDEA) is passed.

1990: The Americans with Disabilities Act (ADA) is signed into law.

2003: In *Grutter v. Bollinger*, the Supreme Court upholds affirmative action admissions.
2009: The Matthew Shepard and James Byrd, Jr. Hate Crimes Prevention Act is signed into law.
2010: The Affordable Care Act (ACA) is signed into law.
2015: The Supreme Court in *Obergefell v. Hodges* rules that the fundamental right to marry is guaranteed to same-sex couples.

DEI-Restrictivist Milestones

1830: Indian Removal Act is signed into law by President Andrew Jackson, leading to the forced relocation of Native American tribes, known as the Trail of Tears.
1882: Chinese Exclusion Act is signed into law, prohibiting all immigration of Chinese laborers to the United States.
1896: *Plessy v. Ferguson*: The Supreme Court upholds the constitutionality of racial segregation under the "separate but equal" doctrine.
1917–1924: A series of Immigration Acts (including the Emergency Quota Act of 1921 and Immigration Act of 1924) impose strict quotas on immigrants based on nationality, largely favoring Northern European immigrants and severely limiting others.
1942: Japanese Internment during WWII: President Franklin D. Roosevelt signs Executive Order 9066, which leads to the forced relocation and internment of Japanese Americans.
1956–1965: The era of Jim Crow laws, state and local laws that enforced racial segregation in the Southern United States, and systemic disenfranchisement of black-racialized Americans through literacy tests, poll taxes, and other tactics.
1981: Philadelphia Order is challenged and significantly weakened, undermining affirmative action policies related to government contractors and employment.
2006: In *Parents Involved in Community Schools v. Seattle School District No. 1*, the Supreme Court rules that public schools cannot seek to achieve or maintain integration through measures that take explicit account of a student's race.

DEI-Expansive or DEI-Restrictive?

2023: The Supreme Court rules that colleges and universities can no longer take race into consideration as a specific basis in admissions – a landmark decision that overturns long-standing precedent that benefited black- and Latino-identified students in higher education.

This extremely controversial decision, while bemoaned as restrictive, may ultimately prove to be a catalyst for selection processes that are more expansivist than the affirmative action policies that allowed race to serve as a selection criterion or factor. Because using the false concept of race perpetuates false distinctions, no longer being able to use it creates a space in which racialization and its effects can become the proper focus.

As illustrated by the American DEI milestones, diversity, equity, and inclusivity are ongoing issues that require continuous effort and attention at all levels of human interaction. In light of these points, arguments that position DEI as anti-American can be recognized as themselves being at odds with the foundational principles and aspirations of the United States. Far from being anti-American, DEI can be seen as a pathway to fulfil the nation's most deeply held values and aspirations. This corrective perspective turns the notion of DEI as anti-American on its head, reframing the commitment to DEI as profoundly and patriotically American.

Why, Then, the Pretense of a Pro-DEI versus Anti-DEI Conflict?

In light of the abundant evidence that DEI is a human universal occupation, no one can actually be against DEI, and either one is DEI-expansivist or DEI-restrictivist, why, then, is there such a pronounced presentation of a pro- and anti-DEI struggle? Here are some reasons why some people assert an anti-DEI stance.

Misunderstanding or Lack of Information: Some people may claim to be against DEI due to misconceptions or a lack of understanding about what DEI actually involves. They might equate DEI initiatives with perceived negative outcomes, such as "reverse discrimination" or unfair advantages for certain groups.

Cognitive Dissonance: Some people experience information about social identity, social bias, and social justice as unfamiliar and in conflict with their own conceptualizations or preferences. This feeling of having to decide whether current beliefs and attitudes or the new contrary (dissonant) information should prevail can lead some people to reject new information (no matter its validity) and maintain or even intensify their convictions.

Perceived Threat to Status Quo: For some individuals, DEI might be seen as a challenge to existing power structures and hierarchies, which they may feel benefit them or align with their worldview.

Political and Ideological Reasons: Opposition to DEI may be rooted in political or ideological stances. Some people may view DEI as being aligned with political ideologies that they oppose.

Cultural or Traditional Beliefs: Some people may feel that DEI conflicts with their cultural, religious, or traditional beliefs and values.

Fear of Change: Some opposition may stem from a general resistance to change. DEI initiatives often involve changes to policies, practices, and cultures, and this can be uncomfortable for those accustomed to the way things have been.

Negative Distortion of DEI: In some cases, opposition may stem from observing poorly executed DEI initiatives that led to unintended negative consequences, causing people to generalize these specific failures to DEI as a whole.

Deliberate Effort to Discredit DEI: Opposition to DEI, in some cases, can be seen as part of a broader, more cynical strategy to delegitimize the entire effort. This strategy doesn't necessarily engage with the specifics of DEI initiatives, but instead aims to discredit the concept as a whole, often by associating it with extreme positions or negative outcomes. Techniques employed to this end include the following:

- Propaganda and Demagoguery: This strategy involves portraying DEI as unappealing and worthy of ridicule and rejection. By associating DEI with extreme positions or perceived negative outcomes (such as reverse discrimination, divisiveness, or an attack on free speech), critics can create a hostile or suspicious environment around DEI efforts without necessarily engaging with the substance of what DEI initiatives are aiming to accomplish.
- Reduction to Absurdity: Critics employing this strategy might take the principles of DEI to an extreme and implausible endpoint to argue that the entire concept is unreasonable. This doesn't engage with the practical and nuanced ways in which DEI is often applied, but aims to paint the entire effort as radical without any virtue.
- Misrepresentation of Intent: Another tactic might involve misrepresenting the intent behind DEI initiatives, framing them as a form of favoritism, indoctrination, or an attack on particular groups, rather than as efforts to foster equal opportunity and create inclusive environments. This kind of portrayal sidesteps the real and substantive goals of DEI and repositions it as something nefarious.
- Political Weaponization: In some cases, opposition to DEI may be politically motivated and used as a rallying point to mobilize certain voter bases. This could involve framing DEI as part of an opposing political agenda and using it to stoke fears or grievances, even when the actual DEI initiatives in question are non-partisan and aimed at fostering equality and inclusion.
- Diverting from Substantive Issues: By creating a heated and polarized debate around DEI itself, critics can shift the conversation away

from specific, substantive issues of inequality and discrimination that DEI efforts aim to address. This can be a way to avoid confronting uncomfortable truths about existing inequities and injustices.

- ♦ Euphemization of Unbecoming Beliefs: To "euphemize" means to express something in milder terms to make it seem less unpleasant or more palatable. When individuals cloak specific biases or prejudices under a broader umbrella of being "anti-DEI," they are essentially softening or masking their true sentiments, making them more socially acceptable or less confrontational. After all, while it might be more to the point of what concerns some people to simply and unabashedly say they object to education about or protection of people with non-binary gender identities or non-cis sexual orientation identities because they believe there is something wrong with such ways of being, doing so would shift the anti-DEI presentation to an anti-some-fellow-humans issue.

These strategies can be very effective, especially in a highly charged political environment where nuanced discussion is often overshadowed by sensational headlines and sound bites. It is a cynical approach, as it seeks to shut down conversation and action around DEI without engaging with the core issues at hand.

This kind of rhetorical strategy seeks not to critique or improve DEI initiatives but to undermine the legitimacy and intent of DEI as a whole, thereby excusing individuals or institutions from having to engage with the principles of diversity, equity, and inclusivity in a meaningful way. Such a strategy cannot help but be hypocritical since it unavoidably represents a DEI stance in and of itself, albeit a severely restrictivist one.

Chapter 1 Summary

DEI is not an 'optional extra' in human interaction but a fundamental aspect of our social existence. DEI is not a binary choice but a spectrum of practice that varies in its expansiveness or restrictiveness.

When individuals or groups position themselves as being 'against DEI,' they are, in fact, advocating for a particular vision of diversity, equity, and inclusivity – one that may favor existing power structures, certain cultural norms, or specific groups of people. In this way, they are not truly outside of the DEI conversation; rather, they are active participants advocating for a specific, more restrictive vision.

Every social decision, whether personal or policy-level, involves considerations of diversity, equity, and inclusivity. Whether one is advocating for change or for maintaining the status quo, those are decisions about how to handle diversity within a community or organization. Opposing DEI initiatives is, therefore, a DEI stance in itself – one that often seeks to preserve existing structures and systems, which may or may not be equitable.

Chapter 1 Reflection and Praxis Prompts

Reflection Prompts

1. Reflect on any misconceptions you may have had about DEI. How did these shape your approach to DEI in your educational practice? Discuss the impact of clarifying these misconceptions on your role as an educator.
2. Consider the ways in which DEI is integral to your daily interactions with students and colleagues. Can you identify an instance where a deeper understanding of DEI could have improved a learning opportunity or interaction?
3. Reflect on your personal stance towards DEI. Do you lean more towards an expansivist or a restrictivist approach? How does this self-awareness influence your teaching and interaction with students of diverse backgrounds?

Praxis Prompts

1. Guide students in understanding how DEI is an essential part of societal interactions and growth.
2. Facilitate a conversation with your class about current DEI-related news, using the chapter's perspective that everyone is inherently a practitioner of DEI.
3. Collaborate with your fellow educators to review your school's policies through the lens of DEI-expansivism.
4. Discuss whether the policies support an expansivist approach, and identify areas where the school can be more inclusive and equitable.
5. Develop a classroom project in which students research and present on historical DEI milestones. This could be a timeline, a

series of presentations, or a debate. The aim is to contextualize DEI as an ongoing process rather than a static concept.
6. Invite students to reflect on the implications of their DEI learning on their sense of self and their interactions with others. Encourage them to journal or create a personal action plan on how they might apply their understanding of DEI principles to foster more inclusive and respectful environments in their own lives, without prescribing specific actions or viewpoints. This exercise aims to promote introspection and personal growth rather than outward advocacy.
7. Reflect on how the foundational understanding of DEI, as presented in this chapter, could support you in conversations with parents who may be resistant to DEI-expansivist approaches. How might you use this information to facilitate a constructive dialogue that acknowledges their concerns while also sharing the universal aspects of DEI that are present in everyday human interactions?
8. Consider role-playing scenarios or creating a guide with key talking points that respect diverse viewpoints while emphasizing the integral role of DEI in education.

Notes

1 Cambridge University Press. (n.d.). Diversity, equity and inclusion. In *Cambridge Advanced Learner's Dictionary & Thesaurus*. Retrieved March 11, 2021, from https://dictionary.cambridge.org/us/dictionary/english/diversity-equity-and-inclusion
2 Cambridge University Press. (n.d.). H2O. In *Cambridge Advanced Learner's Dictionary & Thesaurus*. Retrieved March 11, 2021, from https://dictionary.cambridge.org/us/dictionary/english/h2o?q=H2O
3 Cambridge University Press. (n.d.). Equality, diversity and inclusion. In *Cambridge Advanced Learner's Dictionary & Thesaurus*. Retrieved March 11, 2021, from https://dictionary.cambridge.org/us/dictionary/english/equality-diversity-and-inclusion
4 Garner, D. (2021, January 28). Let's become more divided: In this time of hyperpartisanship, leave it to writers to put us all into pens. *The New York Times*. Retrieved from https://www.nytimes.com/2021/01/28/opinion/Two-types-of-people.html

2

A Framework for Diversity Without Divisiveness

> **Chapter 2 Quick Capture**
>
> *Whoever you are, however you are, you are safe here.*
> ***There but for a change of circumstance, go I.***
>
> If a group does not acknowledge the inevitable diversity of humanity within it, and take measures to ensure that every member is safe to peacefully, civilly, equitably, and inclusively live their personhood, then it is not truly safe for anyone.

Part One – DEI is essential to Education

What is the purpose of education? If you were tasked with providing the best possible answer to that question, what would you come up with? Would your definition emphasize preparation for successful employment, good citizenship, critical thinking, building character, or some other core goal or goals?

It is, of course, crucial that those who invest in the provision of education have a clear sense of the aims of education. And given the diversity of human minds, perspectives, and circumstances, it's natural that different people at different times living in different conditions will arrive at different dispositions about the purpose of education.

What has always been and will always be constant in any and all education processes is the interactive elements of diversity, equity, and inclusion.

Whether in a nursery school, a private elementary-middle school for all genders, a charter high school for black-identified males, an elite college or university, or biology lab where Ph.D. students pursue new understandings and cures for terrible diseases, who is in the room (diversity), what they are provided (equity), and their sense of belonging (inclusivity) will always be crucial factors to how education processes play out.

Even if one were to go about acquiring knowledge and skills exclusively by learning from an artificial intelligence system of instruction and training in complete isolation from other humans, the programing of the system must inevitably root back to human beings who were inescapably influenced by their preferences, values, worldviews, and ideology regarding diversity, equity, and inclusivity. The human variable is an inextricable and essential aspect of education, therefore learning about the concepts and dynamics that pertain to the diversity of ways humans conceive and interact with the world is crucial to learning about anything else.

The diverse tapestry of human experience inevitably colors even the most ostensibly neutral educational content. Thus, the task of learning invariably entails grappling with the myriad dimensions of human diversity. Engaging with this complexity is not a peripheral chore but a core facet of understanding any subject deeply. As educators and learners, the recognition and incorporation of DEI principles within the learning environment is indispensable. By doing so, we acknowledge that every educational act is a reflection of human choices, beliefs, preferences, and biases.

Education has been a subject of debate among philosophers, educators, and policymakers for centuries, reflecting the diversity of human perspectives.

Varied perspectives underscore the concept that educational aims are deeply rooted in one's worldview. They demonstrate that education is about more than the acquisition of knowledge; it's about shaping individuals and societies in ways that reflect our deepest values and beliefs. Diversity in educational philosophy is thus inevitable, highlighting the importance of integrating DEI to address and honor the multifaceted nature of human existence and thought.

Today's debates around diversity in education often center on how schools should address the historical and contemporary experiences of different social identity groups. Parents and political figures alike are deeply divided. Some argue for a curriculum that promotes a diverse and inclusive history that recognizes the contributions and struggles of all groups. Others express concern that such approaches might instill a sense of guilt or discomfort among certain student groups, or that it might lead to what they perceive as a divisive focus on differences rather than commonalities.

This debate itself is an example of the very diversity in perspectives that DEI seeks to understand and navigate. Proponents of DEI-expansivism in education recognize that understanding diversity and the dynamics of social identities is crucial to preparing students to live and work in a multicultural world. Doing so fosters empathy, critical thinking, and a more nuanced understanding of the world. In contrast, DEI-restrictivists may view these efforts as potentially sowing division rather than unity, or prioritizing social issues over academic fundamentals.

The core of the contention rests on differing views about the role of education in society: Is it to preserve and pass on values and knowledge? Is it to prepare students for a globalized world? Or is it to act as a tool for social change and progress? The debate is ongoing, underpinning the essential need for education to grapple with these questions, as they are fundamental to understanding the complex, diverse society in which we live.

What is beyond dispute is the integral role that DEI plays in education. Here are just some of the ways in which DEI is inextricably part of education.

Relevance to Student Engagement: Studies show that when students feel represented and valued, their engagement and participation increase. Without considering DEI, educators may unintentionally create environments where certain students are marginalized, leading to lower engagement and academic performance.

Preparation for a Global Society: In today's interconnected world, students must learn to navigate and appreciate a diversity of cultures, perspectives, and backgrounds. Education that lacks a DEI focus fails to prepare students for the reality of our global society.

Critical Thinking and Problem Solving: DEI encourages critical thinking by exposing students to multiple perspectives. It challenges them to understand complex social dynamics and develop empathy, enhancing their problem-solving skills in socio-diverse contexts.

Innovation and Creativity: Diverse groups have been shown to be more innovative and creative. An educational approach that embraces DEI fosters these qualities by bringing together a wide range of thoughts and ideas.

Equity in Educational Resources: Access to quality education should not be dependent on a student's background. Without a focus on equity, educational resources can be distributed unevenly, perpetuating cycles of disadvantage.

Inclusive Curriculum: An inclusive curriculum reflects the histories, contributions, and experiences of all groups, which is vital for all students to see themselves in their learning and understand the pluralistic nature of society.

Legal and Ethical Obligations: Public institutions have legal mandates to ensure non-discrimination and equal opportunity. Ignoring DEI can lead to violations of these principles and diminish the integrity of educational institutions.

Part Two – The Need for Clarification and Refinement of DEI Methodology

DEI is sometimes pursued and practiced in a reactive manner. DEI practices are often called into action for powerful reasons having to do with people being discriminated against, marginalized, and oppressed. This "why" of DEI is almost always so urgent that it leads to an immediate engagement in actions aimed at redressing conditions that represent social bias. We urgently mobilize to protest a social bias atrocity. We urgently rally to demonstrate resistance to discriminatory policies. We urgently create campaigns to uplift the downtrodden. We urgently do what feels called for in reaction to harmful inequity.

The "whats" of DEI, however, (the DEI efforts catalyzed by the urgent DEI "whys"), while always well-intentioned, don't always sufficiently attend to the crucial work required to avoid unintended consequences. Too often DEI efforts are myopically focused on the specific manifestation of bias that confronts a specific social identity group, and are carried out by people whose only qualifications might be identifying as members of the specific social identity group who are willing and able to put their shoulder to the wheel. While there have been monumentally important models of DEI efforts that fused urgency with deliberated and effective strategy (e.g., Martin Luther King, Jr.'s nonviolent resistance campaign, and the Students Nonviolent Coordinating Committee to name two), DEI responses since the volcanic social unrest triggered by the murder of George Floyd on May 20, 2020 have very often been characterized by the *urgent-need-quick-and-strong-reaction* model.

What this manner of approaching DEI lacks is sufficient attention to the *"how"* of DEI – the fundamental clarifying, unifying, guiding principles that give rise to effective methodology across all social identity categories and all social bias contexts. What all DEI efforts would benefit from is a clear and adaptable unified and unifying framework for understanding and pursuing DEI. Part Three introduces a unified and unifying framework for DEI practice.

Part Three – A Unified and Unifying Antibias Framework for Understanding and Practicing DEI: The Social Identity Prism

The Social Identity Prism provides a comprehensive framework for understanding the multifaceted nature of social identity, social bias, and social justice. The Social Identity Prism framework improves upon approaches that

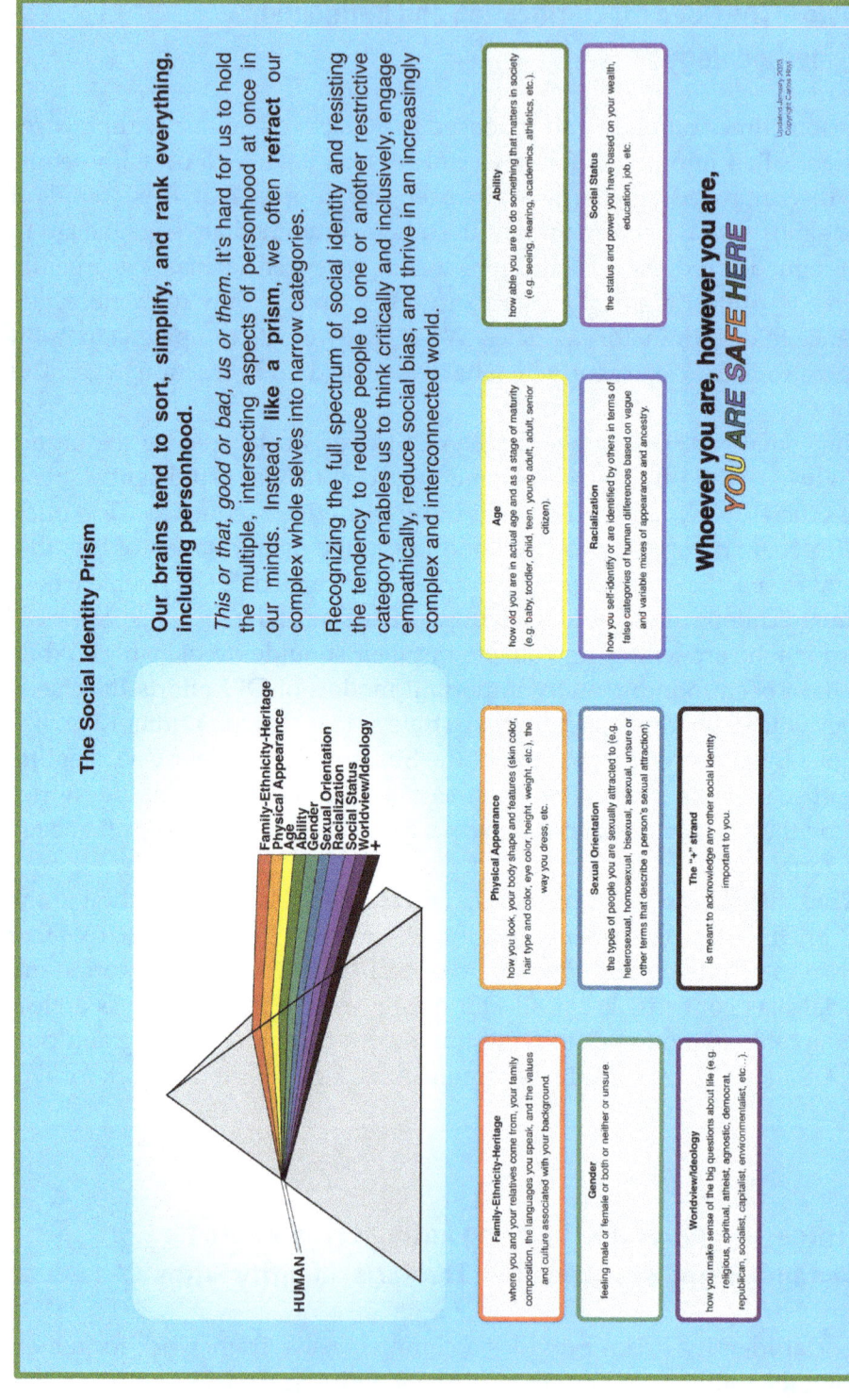

Figure 1.1 The Social Identity Prism

are too often singular-identity focused by providing a wholistic coalitional antibias understanding and approach.

The Social Identity Prism uses the process of light refraction as a metaphor for the how human identity is parsed. Just as a physical prism receives white light, the combination of all of the colors of the spectrum, and diffuses or refracts it so that each color can be viewed separately, so our minds, acting as a psychological prism, perceives human personhood and separates it into all of the social identity categories we are inclined and/or conditioned to detect (Family-Ethnicity-Heritage, Physical Appearance, Age, Ability, Gender, Sexual Orientation, Racialization, Social Status, and Worldview/ Ideology).

The Four Key Components of the Social Identity Prism
1. The prism metaphor, on the left side of the diagram, visualizes how the mind refracts complex, irreducible personhood into common social identity categories.
2. The right side of the diagram explains the universal human tendencies towards categorizing and ranking as ways to makes sense of the world. It also encourages us to try to temper these tendencies to avoid reductive constructions that lead to ignoring what we have in common, including the basic right to be treated equitably and inclusively.
3. The definitions of the social identity categories are included on the diagram to clarify their meanings and to remind us that such clarity is crucial to avoiding confusion and conflict when sharing feelings and thoughts about terms and concepts that, though commonly used, don't always mean the same things to everyone.
4. The declaration "Whoever you are, however you are, you are safe here" encapsulates the tool's purpose: promoting an environment where the peaceful and tolerant expression of one's unique humanity is paramount. It advocates for expansive inclusivity where every person is safe to exist and express their identity without fear of opposition or harm, as long as they equally commit to the safety and tolerance of all others.

The Social Identity Prism represents a synthesis of Social Identity Theory by representing the various dimensions and interplay of an individual's identity within a social context (social versus personal identity). Social Identity Theory, developed by Henri Tajfel and John Turner,[1] posits that a person's sense of who they are is informed and influenced by their group memberships (social identity categories which are assigned/ascribed as well as those which are subscribed to – recognizing that personal and social identity do not always align). The key aspects of this theory are categorized into *cognitive awareness* of the group, *emotional attachment* to the group, and *evaluative significance* of the group membership.

The Social Identity Prism visualizes these categories and provides a framework for understanding and exploring the multifaceted nature of identity. It allows individuals to map out the various groups they subscribe to and are assigned to, recognize the complex interplay between these groups, understand the influence of these group memberships on their behavior and perceptions, and the impact of how they are treated based on how they are perceived vis-à-vis social identity group membership.

In essence, the prism helps to illuminate the dimensions of social identity, offering insights into how these dimensions contribute to an individual's self-concept and social behaviors, and how they translate to how they are treated by others. It reflects the dynamic nature of identity, which can change depending on context and time, and highlights the significance of intersectionality – the way different aspects of a person's social identities are associated with differential social advantages or disadvantages.

By using the Social Identity Prism, educators and students alike can better understand their own identities and those of others, leading to a more nuanced appreciation of diversity and fostering a more inclusive environment. This tool encourages reflection on one's position within social structures and the potential impact on interactions and relationships within the educational setting and beyond.

Key Benefits of the Social Identity Prism Framework include acknowledging the Whole Person: recognizing the multifaceted nature of individual identities, which aligns with contemporary views on intersectionality (which might more accurately be understood as "interfaciality" *. By acknowledging that identities are complex and intertwined, this framework counters reductionist approaches and promotes a nuanced understanding of personal experiences.

* The concept of intersectionality, coined by Kimberlé Crenshaw,[2] used to describe how different social identities interact is actually about *interfacing* social identities, not simply identities that share a point of connection, crossing, or commonality. "Interface" might be a more accurate capture of social identity dynamics that "intersectionality" is meant to describe.

Using "interface" to describe these dynamics emphasizes the active engagement and interaction between different aspects of identity, suggesting a more dynamic process of negotiation and influence rather than static points of overlap. It suggests a continuous process of interaction and exchange where different aspects of identity communicate, influence, and shape experiences in a fluid and evolving manner.

Fostering Intersectional Empathy: a deep understanding of how different social justice movements are interconnected. Interfacial empathy is crucial as it enables individuals and groups to support one another in a united front against common societal issues, rather than in isolated silos.

Promoting Expansive Inclusivity: calls for unity across social identity groups, which is a powerful strategy for amplifying collective voices against systemic bias and oppression. It's a move away from single-issue activism toward a more united and comprehensive form of advocacy.

Avoiding Silos: moving beyond reductive, insular constructions of identity, which often limit antibias efforts to singular identity markers. By promoting inclusive activism, the framework aims to create broader coalitions that recognize the complexity of identities and the shared nature of many social struggles.

Advocating for Inclusive Solutions: promoting policies and practices that consider the diversity within groups, fostering solutions beneficial to a broad coalition. This approach not only supports individual groups but also promotes overall societal progress.

Part Four: The Synergy Between DEI, SEL, and Health & Wellness: Better Together for Learning and Growth

The domains of Social-Emotional Learning (SEL), Health & Wellness (H&W), DEI hold immense potential for synergy and mutual enrichment. By combining their efforts and processes, we can create powerful educational and societal environments that promote both individual well-being and collective progress.

SEL focuses on cultivating social and emotional skills in individuals (i.e., fostering self-awareness, self-management, social awareness, responsible decision-making, and relationship skills.[3] These capacities are essential for developing positive interpersonal relationships, resolving conflicts constructively, and navigating the complexities of social interactions.

Health & Wellness Education focuses on teaching foundational functional health information that support health-enhancing behaviors.[4]

DEI centers on recognizing and valuing diverse human groups and creating inclusive and equitable conditions that activate the benefits of diversity. It facilitates the awareness and dismantling of psychological, structural, and systemic barriers and biases, fostering environments where all individuals are respected, valued, and provided equal opportunities to thrive.

Why DEI Awareness Is Essential to Optimizing SEL Competencies

Each competency within Social-Emotional Learning (SEL) requires an awareness of social bias to ensure that marginalized groups are not excluded from the positive benefits of these competencies. Here's an explanation of how each SEL competency intersects with social bias:

Self-Awareness: Self-awareness involves recognizing and understanding one's own emotions, strengths, limitations, and biases. Awareness of social bias is essential here to prevent unconscious biases from influencing one's perception of oneself and others. It helps individuals reflect on their own privileges and biases, fostering a more accurate understanding of their own identity and how it may impact their interactions with others.

Social Awareness: Social awareness entails understanding and empathizing with the experiences, perspectives, and diversity of others. Recognizing social bias is crucial to develop empathy and to challenge stereotypes and prejudices that might hinder an inclusive understanding of others. By acknowledging and actively seeking to understand different perspectives, individuals can better advocate for marginalized groups and work towards creating inclusive spaces.

Self-Management: Self-management involves regulating emotions, controlling impulses, and adapting to various situations. Awareness of social bias is essential for self-management as it helps individuals recognize and control biases that might lead to discriminatory behaviors or exclusionary practices. It enables individuals to navigate challenging situations while upholding fairness, equity, and inclusion.

Relationship Skills: Relationship skills involve effectively communicating, collaborating, and resolving conflicts with others. Awareness of social bias is crucial in relationship skills, as it allows individuals to navigate power dynamics and address biases that may hinder equitable and respectful interactions. By recognizing and challenging biases, individuals can build meaningful connections, engage in inclusive collaborations, and foster equitable relationships.

Responsible Decision-Making: Responsible decision-making involves making ethical and constructive choices that consider diverse perspectives and consequences. Awareness of social bias is paramount here to ensure that decisions are fair, equitable, and inclusive. It helps individuals critically evaluate the impact of biases on decision-making processes and work towards solutions that promote justice, equality, and the well-being of all.

Why DEI Awareness Is Essential to Optimizing Health & Wellness Education

Taking into account the diversity of any given student group is essential to providing optimal H&W education. Establishing a strong connection between teachers and students, providing curricula that represent both mirrors and windows, tailoring material and approaches to address the unique needs of different social identity populations, and providing support and evaluation methods that are responsive to the circumstances of the group are DEI practices that enhance H&W pedagogy. By combining the power of DEI, SEL, and H&W, the integrated approach fosters inclusive mindsets, social and health competencies, and empathetic engagement, empowering individuals to grow into well-rounded citizens who are able to contribute to a more equitable and interconnected society.

How DEI, SEL, & H&W Educators Can Achieve a Whole Greater Than Its Parts

DEI, SEL, and H&W educators play a vital role in leveraging the benefits of integrated DEI-SEL-H&W approaches. Here are some concrete actions they can take:

Collaborate and Co-plan:
- Work collaboratively with colleagues across DEI, SEL, and H&W disciplines to develop integrated lesson plans and activities.
- Co-plan sessions or workshops that explicitly address how DEI, SEL, and H&W interface and reinforce one another.
- Engage in regular communication and collaboration to align goals and strategies.

Embrace Inclusively Responsive Practices:
- Prioritize cultural responsiveness in teaching and facilitation, acknowledging and valuing the diverse backgrounds and experiences of students.
- Incorporate culturally diverse resources, materials, and examples that reflect students' identities and promote inclusivity.
- Foster a classroom environment that encourages students to share their perspectives and experiences, ensuring that all voices are heard and respected.

Facilitate Identity Exploration and Reflection:
- Create space for students to explore and reflect on their own identities, values, and beliefs, promoting self-awareness and cultural competence.
- Incorporate activities that encourage students to examine and challenge their own biases and assumptions.
- Facilitate discussions that help students understand the intersectionality of identities and the influence of societal structures on individuals and groups.

Promote Inclusive Dialogue and Collaboration:
- Facilitate discussions that encourage respectful dialogue around sensitive topics related to DEI and SEL.
- Foster an inclusive classroom environment where students feel safe to express their thoughts and ask questions.
- Develop collaborative projects and group activities that promote teamwork, empathy, and appreciation of diverse perspectives.
- Model and teach that the ability to build a strong, healthy relationship across all social identities requires a combination of empathy, compassion, and justice.

Professional Development and Continuous Learning:
- Engage in ongoing professional development to deepen knowledge and skills in DEI, SEL, and H&W.
- Attend workshops, conferences, or webinars focused on integrating DEI, SEL, and H&W principles and practices.
- Seek opportunities to learn from experts and share best practices with other educators in the field.

Assess and Reflect:
- Regularly assess and reflect on the effectiveness of integrated DEI-SEL-H&W approaches in meeting the needs of students.
- Collect and analyze data on student outcomes related to inclusivity, and equity, social-emotional development, and Health & Wellness.
- Use assessment findings to inform instructional adjustments and improvements in DEI-SEL-H&W integration efforts.

By taking these concrete actions, DEI, SEL, and H&W educators can leverage the benefits of integrated DEI-SEL-H&W approaches and create transformative learning experiences for their students. A dedication to creating inclusive, equitable, and socially-emotionally supportive environments is instrumental in promoting students' well-being, fostering positive relationships, and preparing them to navigate an increasingly diverse world.

Chapter 2 Summary

The chapter introduces the Social Identity Prism as a tool to understand and navigate the complexities of social identity, bias, and justice, promoting a holistic approach that encourages empathy, inclusive unity, and broad coalitions beyond identity silos. It explores the purpose of education from various historical perspectives, asserting that understanding and applying DEI is essential in all educational processes. Chapter 2 of the book lays out a comprehensive framework for DEI pedagogy in education, emphasizing the importance of integrating DEI with Social-Emotional Learning (SEL) and Health & Wellness (H&W) to foster optimal learning and growth.

Chapter 2 Reflection and Praxis Prompts

Reflection Prompts

1. Reflect on a time when you witnessed or experienced the interconnection of different social justice movements. How did this influence your understanding of the issues at hand?
2. Consider your role in an educational setting. How can you foster interfacial empathy among your students or colleagues to support a united front against societal issues?
3. In what ways can educators and students move beyond single-issue activism to foster a sense of expansive inclusive unity? Provide an example from your own experience.
4. Discuss how inclusive unity can be a powerful strategy in amplifying collective voices against systemic bias and oppression within an educational context.
5. How have you or how could you contribute to creating broader coalitions in your educational environment that recognize the complexity of identities and shared social struggles?
6. What are some potential challenges in moving beyond insular constructions of identity, and how might these be addressed in classroom settings?
7. Discuss how understanding the multifaceted nature of your own identity has affected your approach to teaching and interacting with students.
8. Reflect on how your educational approach prepares students to navigate and appreciate a diversity of cultures, perspectives, and backgrounds.
9. What strategies do you use to enhance critical thinking and problem-solving skills through DEI?

DEI-SEL-H&W Integrative Mindset Development
1. Using the Social Identity Prism framework, map out your own various group memberships and reflect on how they influence your perceptions and behaviors.
2. Reflect on how the integration of DEI, SEL, and H&W principles can shape the learning environment in your classroom.
3. How can you ensure that these principles are not treated as separate entities but as interconnected aspects of student development?
4. Consider a health & wellness curriculum that you are familiar with. How can DEI awareness enhance the delivery of this curriculum to cater to the diverse needs of students?
5. Reflect on how self-awareness and relationship skills taught in SEL can be deepened by including discussions on social identities, biases, and social justice.
6. How can Health & Wellness education be designed to address the unique stressors faced by marginalized groups?

Praxis Prompts
1. Develop a plan that incorporates both physical health and social-emotional support.
2. Design ways to incorporate the understanding of social bias into the teaching of responsible decision-making within SEL programs.
3. Identify strategies you will adopt to continuously develop your ability to effectively integrate DEI, SEL, and H&W in your teaching practice.
4. Design a lesson plan that illustrates how you can integrate DEI principles into SEL activities to promote Health & Wellness among all students.
5. How would you measure the impact of an integrated DEI, SEL, and H&W approach on your students' growth and well-being?

Notes

1 Huddy, L. (2001). From social to political identity: A critical examination of social identity theory. *Political Psychology*, 22(1), 127–156. Retrieved from http://www.jstor.org/stable/3791909

2 Crenshaw, K. (1989). Demarginalizing the intersection of race and sex: A Black feminist critique of antidiscrimination doctrine, feminist theory and antiracist politics. *University of Chicago Legal Forum, 1981*(10), Article 8.
3 Collaborative for Academic, Social, and Emotional Learning (CASEL). (n.d.). *What Is the CASEL Framework?* Retrieved October 3, 2023, from https://casel.org/fundamentals-of-sel/what-is-the-casel-framework/
4 Centers for Disease Control and Prevention. (2019, May 29). *Characteristics of an Effective Health Education Curriculum.* Retrieved October 3, 2023, from https://www.cdc.gov/healthyschools/sher/characteristics/index.htm

3

Reconciling Contested Issues Toward Positive Parent-School Partnership

Chapter 3 Quick Capture
1. School should focus on academics and leave matters concerning values and identity to parents.
2. Devoting resources to DEI takes away from already-limited resources for achieving academic excellence.
3. I deserve to know what you're teaching when it comes to DEI, and have my say about it.
4. I feel like all I hear about when it comes to DEI is race, gender, and sexual orientation. Is that all DEI is about at Our School?
5. DEI makes our American history look like a parade of shame and horror and forces kids to feel like victims or victimizers.
6. Being inclusive should mean respecting *my* values and beliefs, not just those of some people.
7. Equity to create equality of outcomes requires dumbing down expectations and disadvantaging advanced students.
8. Parents should be able to opt out of education about gender and sexual orientation identity because it amounts to sex/sexuality education, and parents have rights to opt out of sex/sexuality education.
9. Placing kids into so-called "affinity groups" is divisive.
10. How is it fair that some identities and cultures are celebrated at school and others ignored?

> 11. What if I simply can't abide some DEI practices at Our School that I feel disrespect and defy my right to say what my child will and will not be exposed to?
>
> Thoughtful, non-partisan, effective DEI pedagogy and practice must anticipate and provide clear answers to the *why*, *what*, and *how* questions some parents have about DEI's purpose and methods.

This chapter recognizes that many parents have doubts about DEI's purpose and practices. In this chapter, each of the common questions, concerns, and complaints about perceptions of DEI's purpose and practices will be addressed. In some cases, an example of a letter to parents or a policy statement (for the fictitious "Our School") that can be adapted to the specific circumstances of a given school is provided. In all cases, the aim is to provide clear, constructive, and definitive responses to the hot-button issues that surround DEI pedagogy and practice.

The chapter begins with a corrective, connective framing of the currently popularly used phrase "parents' rights." "Parents' Rights!" has become a rallying cry around several contentious issues in the educational and political spheres. It is often invoked by those who believe that parental authority should be paramount in decisions affecting their children's upbringing, education, and welfare. "Parents' rights" has been employed to advocate for restrictions in what can be included in educational curriculum, particularly regarding race, gender, sexual orientation, and sexuality.

The rallying cry of "parents' rights" is a call for increased parental control and influence over the environments and systems that children are part of. It often stems from a desire to protect children from what some parents perceive as negative external influences, coupled with the belief that they, as parents, know what is best for their child's development and moral education. The term has become politically charged, with significant debate over the balance between parental rights, children's rights, societal interests, and the professional judgment of educators and administrators.

In an effort to reframe and defuse "parents' rights" as a signal for and symbol of division and conflict, this chapter begins with an inclusive take on every parent's rights and a letter to parents of the fictitious "Our School" that clarifies its approach to DEI. The chapter then continues with material that addresses the 11 common questions and concerns.

Part One – Every Parent's Rights

Parents are bound to have disagreements about all kinds of things from philosophies of life to day-to-day practicalities, but it shouldn't be hard to find common ground in our fundamental concerns about our kids' safety and welfare.

Some parents reading this have a child who is left-handed in a world built for people who are right-handed. These parents have every right to expect that their child will not be forced to learn to write or throw or eat with the hand that feels "right" for everyone else.

Some parents reading this have a child whose abilities and learning style diverge from most students. These parents have every right to expect that their child will not be teased or ostracized or labelled, or treated as lazy, incompetent, or unworthy of equitable care and support, and, instead, to expect that their child will receive what they need to learn and thrive.

Some parents reading this have children who observe religious and/or cultural customs that are central to their sense of family and heritage but are not considered mainstream holidays. These parents have every right to expect that their child will be released from regular school expectations while observing traditions that are every bit as important as those officially observed by the school.

Some parents reading this have a child whose gender identity does not align with the assumptions some people make about them. These parents have as much of a right to expect that their child will not be misgendered as do parents of children who have binary gender identities.

Some parents reading this have children whose ethnicity, racialization, sexual orientation, social status, or worldview is treated as a reason to tease, exclude, or otherwise mistreat them. These parents have every right to expect that their child will be provided with equitable protection, regard, encouragement, support, and love through policies, pedagogy, programs, people, and environments that reflect their worth and worthiness.

Every parent reading this has every right to expect that their child's school understands the crucial connection between fostering a sense of belonging and equipping students to excel academically and prosper in an increasingly diverse and interconnected global community.

Whatever disagreements we might have as parents trying to look out for our kids, navigating those differences respectfully, constructively, and inclusively is easier when we first recognize and uphold our shared parents' rights.

Part Two – Our School's Diversity, Equity, and Inclusivity Principles and Practices: A Model Letter to Parents of "Our School"

Dear Our School Parent,

At Our School, we recognize the demonstrated fact that diversity is a strength and that promoting equity and inclusivity is essential for creating a safe, welcoming, and successful learning environment.

Our DEI practices are designed to help students understand and appreciate the full range of human diversity, promote respect, empathy, and understanding across all forms of social identities, and prosper in an increasingly interconnected world.

We recognize that DEI is an area of education and care that involves matters related to identity, culture, beliefs and values – topics that are important to parenting practices and preferences. This being the case, DEI-related education benefits greatly from a clear and strong home-school partnership. We welcome open, honest, and constructive dialogue related to DEI as the best way to foster understanding, confidence, and collaboration.

Our DEI Principles and Practices are presented here in response to a to series of questions and concerns some parents have expressed about DEI at Our School. They are meant to provide clarity and guidance on how we approach DEI education, how we respond to inquiries and concerns, and how we can maintain respectful and constructive engagement.

We encourage all parents to review these guidelines carefully and to reach out to us if they have any questions or concerns. We are committed to working together with you to create a learning environment that is inclusive, respectful, supportive, and joyful for all students.

Thank you for your ongoing support and partnership.

Your Truly,

Principal, Our School

Diversity, Equity, and Inclusion Principles and Practices – Questions/Concerns and Responses

Questions/Concerns #1: School Should Focus on Academics and Leave Matters Concerning Values and Identity to Parents

Response

The mandate for schools to focus on academics is clear and unequivocal. However, the comprehensive education of a child extends beyond academic knowledge and skills. Schools are charged with the task of preparing young people not just for college and careers but also for the roles they will play as members of a diverse and democratic society.

An integral part of this preparation involves equipping students with the ability to understand and navigate social complexities, including those related to identity. The reason is twofold: first, discrimination and bias can and do impede the academic and social-emotional development of students; second, schools are microcosms of the larger society and therefore reflect its diversity and complexities.

Anti-discrimination and antibias education in schools help students develop critical thinking skills, empathy, and a sense of justice. It contributes to creating a school culture that respects and values diversity, thereby fostering an environment where all students feel safe, included, and able to learn. Such education does not impose specific values or prefer specific identities, but rather encourages understanding and respect for different perspectives, preparing students to live and work in a pluralistic society.

Additionally, schools must adhere to legal and ethical obligations to protect students from discrimination and harassment. Ignoring these obligations can create an environment where bullying and prejudice go unchallenged, negatively impacting student well-being and learning.

While it is true that parents are the primary educators of their children regarding values and identity, schools play a complementary role by providing a broader social context. Education about anti-discrimination and antibias supports the development of well-rounded individuals who can contribute positively to society and the world at large.

Thus, while schools must focus on academic excellence, they must also attend to the social and emotional development and antibias capacities of their students, as all are essential for the growth of informed, responsible, and compassionate citizens.

Inclusivity Is a Legal Requirement

There are a number of federal, state, and local laws, regulations, and expectations that require anti-discrimination/antibias education. Public schools have a legal responsibility to provide an inclusive and safe environment for all students. Several federal laws require this commitment to inclusivity:

Title VI of the Civil Rights Act of 1964: Prohibits discrimination on the basis of race, color, or national origin in programs and activities receiving federal financial assistance.

Title IX of the Education Amendments Act of 1972: Prohibits sex-based discrimination in any school or any other education program that receives funding from the federal government. This is also applied to protect students from discrimination based on gender identity and sexual orientation.

Individuals with Disabilities Education Act (IDEA) passed in 1975: Requires public schools to provide free and appropriate education to students with disabilities, including customizing educational plans to meet the needs of each child.

Section 504 of the Rehabilitation Act of 1973: Ensures that individuals with disabilities have equal access to education, employment, and various public services. It requires schools to provide appropriate accommodations and modifications for students with disabilities.

The Equal Access Act of 1984: Requires that federally funded secondary schools provide equal access to extracurricular clubs and activities, regardless of the religious, political, philosophical, or other content of the speech at such meetings.

These laws collectively underscore the obligation of public schools to foster an environment where students from all backgrounds have equal access to education without fear of discrimination. They are designed not to impose values or ideologies but to guarantee rights and provide a safe and equitable educational experience for every student.

Preventing Bullying Requires Antibias Education

Schools are generally required to address bullying. The specific requirements can vary depending on the state and local laws, as well as the policies of individual school districts. Most states have laws that mandate schools to have anti-bullying policies and procedures in place.

These typically include requirements for the following:

Prevention: Implementing programs or curricula aimed at educating students about bullying and its effects. Prevention strategies can also include creating a positive school climate that discourages bullying.

Intervention: Taking immediate action when bullying is observed or reported. This can involve direct intervention with the students involved and may include counseling, behavioral management plans, or disciplinary actions.

Adjudication: Following a formal process to review reported incidents of bullying, which can involve investigations and determining appropriate consequences for the behavior.

Reporting: Establishing clear procedures for students, staff, and parents to report bullying incidents. Schools are often required to document these incidents and may need to report them to state education departments.

Training: Providing training for staff and students on identifying, preventing, and responding to bullying.

Support: Offering support to victims of bullying, which can include counseling services or accommodations to ensure their safety and well-being at school.

The specific details and robustness of these requirements can differ widely. Some states have very comprehensive anti-bullying laws, while others may have less prescriptive guidelines. Additionally, at the federal level, while there is no singular anti-bullying law, schools are required under various civil rights laws to address and prevent harassment that is based on protected characteristics such as race, sex, disability, and national origin, as failure to do so may be a violation of students' civil rights.

Education against social bias is a critical component of bullying prevention. Many incidents of bullying are rooted in biases – conscious or unconscious – against individuals or groups based on characteristics such as ethnicity, heritage, physical appearance, age, ability, gender, sexual orientation, racialization, social status, and worldview. Recognizing and addressing these biases are essential steps in creating a school environment that is safe and inclusive for all students.

Schools have a responsibility to implement comprehensive antibias education programs that do the following:

Raise Awareness: Educate students, staff, and the school community about the various forms of social bias and discrimination, and how these can lead to bullying and exclusion.

Promote Empathy and Respect: Through classroom discussions, assemblies, and school-wide initiatives, encourage students to develop empathy, respect differences, and appreciate the value of diversity.

Encourage Critical Thinking: Help students to critically analyze stereotypes and prejudices that they may encounter in media, textbooks, and even in casual conversations, and understand the harm they cause.

Develop Social-Emotional Skills: Integrate social-emotional learning (SEL) into the curriculum to equip students with skills such as emotional regulation, perspective-taking, and relationship-building, which can help reduce bias-based bullying.

Empower Bystanders: Train students on how to safely stand up against bullying and support their peers, transforming them from passive bystanders into active upstanders.

Provide Support Systems: Establish clear support mechanisms for students who are victims of bias and bullying, including counseling services and safe spaces where they can report and discuss incidents.

Involve the Community: Engage parents and the broader community in conversations and trainings about bias and bullying, ensuring that these efforts are supported both in and out of school.

Model Inclusive Behavior: School leaders and staff must lead by example, demonstrating inclusive behavior and responding to bias and bullying incidents appropriately.

By addressing social bias directly and comprehensively, schools can not only reduce instances of bullying but also create an educational environment that fosters mutual understanding, respect, and equality. This aligns with the federal and state mandates for educational institutions to ensure that all students have equal access to educational opportunities in a safe and nondiscriminatory environment.

Parents who object to education that includes recognition of and respect for the wide range of identities represented in any student body on the basis of concern about a political or ideological agenda are encouraged to recognize the nonpartisan legal requirements that underpin such education.

Inclusive education is not a matter of choice or agenda. It is not negotiable. It is imperative.

Questions/Concerns #2: Devoting Resources to DEI Takes Away from Already-Limited Resources for Achieving Academic Excellence

Response

The value of diversity, equity, and inclusivity: We recognize that diversity is a strength and that promoting equity and inclusion is essential for creating a safe and welcoming learning environment for all students. Our DEI practices are designed to help students understand and appreciate the full range of human diversity, promote respect, empathy, and positive interaction across all forms of social identities, and prosper in an increasingly interconnected world.

- We also acknowledge the evidence that diversity, equity, and inclusivity (where inclusivity involves a sense of belonging) are not only compatible with academic success, they enhance it. Concerns that paying attention to DEI might somehow detract from academic excellence are not validated by growing evidence that when students feel welcome, safe, respected, and a good sense of belonging, they do better in terms of schoolwork, mental health, and behavior.
- It is certainly true that channeling some of Our School's resources (money, people, time, etc.) toward DEI education and enrichment must technically result in having less resources for other investments. However, it's important to not fall into a zero-sum game attitude about this, one that concludes and bemoans that resources devoted to DEI must be taken directly from other areas of our educational programs and activities.
- We have been successful in acquiring grant funding for DEI initiatives which allow us to avoid reducing resources committed to other areas.
- We have always devoted resources to areas of our educational program that are not strictly "academic" but nonetheless essential to creating and maintaining a community in which students feel safe, seen, welcome, and happy enough to fully engage in academic endeavor. As noted elsewhere in the document, DEI done well is a proven essential component of creating and maintaining such a community. To put it plainly, resources dedicated to DEI represent money and time well spent.

Questions/Concerns #3: I Deserve to Know What You're Teaching When It Comes to DEI, and Have My Say About It

Response
Communication and transparency: We believe that providing wide-open windows into all of our practices, including DEI, is good for everyone. We will always be happy to let parents know what we're doing in the classroom in terms of materials, methods, and rationales.

Formal programs for sharing information related to our educational programs and practices will be provided periodically using in-person and video meeting formats in order to maximize the opportunity for all parents to participate, and to make it possible to create structures that maximize safety and equitable use of question-and-answer periods.

Questions or concerns about diversity, equity, and inclusivity
- Parents who have concerns that anything occurring in our educational programs has resulted in harm are strongly encouraged to contact school leaders with the details of their concerns.
- Questions or concerns about how antibias education is approached can and should be expressed if there is a sincere desire to gain clarifying information.
- Questions about the need for or validity of inclusive education (DEI) per se amount to questions that have been asked and answered in the form of easily accessible federal, state, and local laws, regulations, and expectations.

Hearsay, anonymous reports, and unfounded complaints
- We cannot respond to reports by a community member about how other community members feel about any given matter. Individuals are entitled and encouraged to represent their own views and avoid speaking for others in the absence of clear authorization from others.
- We cannot respond to anonymous expressions that may or may not represent actual district members. We will respond to inquiries and concerns of individuals who identify themselves and contact school personal and leadership directly.
- We cannot respond to complaints that amount to worry or predictions or even convictions that something happening at school is "harmful" or "bad" without any evidence of harm or what is actually negative about the subject of the concern.

How we talk with one another: basic human dignity and decency
- We affirm and uphold the basic human dignity of all people and the right of every person to be treated civilly and respectfully, even and especially in the context of disagreement.
- We are empathic regarding any upset and even anger that can accompany a parent's sense of obligation to protect their children from any values, beliefs, or practice they perceive to be contrary to their worldviews.
- At the same time, we denounce personal attacks and reject them as valid bases for engagement.

- We will always be willing and available to engage in civil and constructive dialogue about any matter at Our School.
- Just as we would not tolerate your child or you being subjected to offensive or aggressive behavior in our community, we will not subject our teachers or any employee at Our School to such behavior.

Questions/Concerns #4: I Feel Like All I Hear about When It Comes to DEI Is Race, Gender, and Sexual Orientation. Is That All DEI Is about at Our School?

Response
As explained and emphasized in the Social Identity Prism and the Cauldron of Social Bias, Our School recognizes the need to pursue inclusivity inclusively.

- Our School's approach to DEI emphasizes antibias education and practice. The term "antibias" encompasses the full range of ways that human differences and similarities can result in powerful positive connections and also serve as the basis of social bias.
- Approaches to DEI work that focus narrowly on one category of social identity run the risk of reducing the complexity of personhood. No one is just their family-ethnicity-heritage, or just their physical appearance or age, or ability, and so on. We are all all of our identities all of the time.
- There are good reasons to address social bias issues that are directed at people perceived to be members of a particular social identity group. Opposing racism, genderism, homophobia, ableism, lookism, ethnocentrism, classism, ageism, and worldview intolerance (with the exception of opposing intolerant worldviews) will always be called for and important, but doing so in ways that do not neglect the whole-person reality of the circumstance is both possible and necessary to avoid divisiveness and at least the impression of ignoring some social identities.

Questions/Concerns #5: DEI Makes Our American History Look Like a Parade of Shame and Horror, and It Forces Kids to Feel Like Victims or Victimizers

Response
The study of controversial/challenging topics: Controversy is not in and of itself something to be avoided. Topics that might be considered by some to be controversial are bound to be part of the educational process (whether in the context of English, history, social studies, the arts, or any other study area).

The study of topics related to discrimination, oppression, and injustice can and should be conducted based on facts and free of implication that students should feel blame, shame, guilt, or virtue based on their social identities.

At Our School we provide students with the following statements of clarification and confidence about how we should talk when we talk about social identity, social bias, and social justice, and how we should feel when we study historical incidences of social bias. We hope these statements will leave parents comforted and confident about the way we fulfil our responsibility to provide factual information about significant historical issues related to social identity, social bias, and social justice.

How Should We Talk When We Talk about Social Identity?

1. *Your identity is the way you answer the question "who are you?"*

Your identity is actually *many identities* because you can answer that question in many ways. When we talk about social identity, we mean the ways each person defines their sense of social identity group membership and the ways others see them (which may not always match).

Feeling that we belong to a group often helps us feel proud, grounded, and protected (like being part of a team). Sometimes feeling that we're part of an *US*-group can lead to us to think and act negatively towards people we see as belonging to a *THEM*-group. Sadly, sometimes people are treated unjustly just because of the group they belong to or are thought to belong to.

Sometimes the groups we choose to be part of match up with the groups others think we are part of. Sometimes they don't. For example, someone might look at you and guess that you have a certain ethnicity (where you and your family come from), and they might be right or they might be wrong.

Only you can say for sure what your identities are. Social identity is a tricky thing. We tend to perceive people (ourselves included sometimes!) *prismatically* (as if we can neatly mark where one identity starts and where another ends), but perhaps we should recognize that our complex selves are better understood as being *kaleidoscopic* (a brilliant confluence of everything we feel ourselves to be).

2. *Talking about social identity as scholars, not necessarily as representatives*

We'll learn and talk about a lot of things that involve social identity. When we do, let's think back to the Social Identity Prism and remember that everyone is a whole person who really can't be and really shouldn't be reduced to a single identity, and a person's identities should never lead us to think less of them.

Let's also remember that when we study and talk about social identity – when it comes up in a book or movie or the news or some other way, we'll be learning how humans *in general* think about social identity; we won't necessarily talk about how any individual in our group thinks about their own social identity. Students might choose to share things about themselves, but we shouldn't and won't expect anyone to do that.

One way to think about our approach to studying social identity is to think of the difference between *religious study* and *the study of religion*. In the first case, the participants' personal beliefs or faith is something to be shared and known by everyone in the group. In the second case, the focus is not personal belief or faith but, instead, exploring and understanding how human beings engage in religious thinking and behavior. In that case, the participants' personal views might be discussed if they choose to discuss them, but that wouldn't be expected and wouldn't be central to the experience.

3. <u>Let's not make it weird</u>

It can feel weird to be in a group discussing a particular social identity and see everyone looking at you or expecting you to explain what it's like to be part of that group just because folks assume you are a member. We don't want to put anyone in that awkward situation.

4. <u>An Advisory for Scholars: How Should We Feel When We Study Historic and Current Instances of Social Bias?</u>

As scholars, we will explore crucial facts about human history and American history, some of which illuminate the ways in which people and events have strayed from ideals of fairness, liberty, and the pursuit of happiness.

We will study how Columbus invaded this continent, the deadly Trail of Tears, the horrific Middle Passage, the unthinkable Holocaust, and how the interaction between social identity, social bias, and social justice can result in atrocity.

These things are real and have shaped the world and our lives no less than natural disasters or pandemics, and no less than the amazingly positive things that have characterized human existence. We ignore them at our peril because they represent negative patterns of social conduct that will only change through discernment, disruption, and preventative measures going forward.

When we learn about people who acted in ways that represent a disregard for human dignity, it will be important not to fall into the trap of thinking that people who share outward characteristics are bound to be alike in terms of their conduct.

When we study how the world has come to be as it is (the good, the bad, and the ugly), we are not blaming people here and now for what happened there and then, and we are not condemning people to continue bad patterns; we are freeing and empowering everyone to make their own decisions.

Genes + Environment + Chance + Choice = YOU. You are a complicated, intersectional, volitional being. You cannot be reduced to some essentialized human type whose behavior is predictably good or bad or who is virtuous or guilty by association with others with whom you share social identity categories.

Let's consider this the land of the free enough to pursue the truth and the brave enough to face it together.

Questions/Concerns #6: Being Inclusive Should Mean Respecting My Values and Beliefs, Not Just Those of Some People

Response
Creating a healthy tension between personal beliefs *and* public tolerance: Members of our community are entitled to their *personal beliefs* and, at the same time, expected to practice *public tolerance* of diversity. A truly inclusive community welcomes diversity of worldviews and ideology and, at the same time, requires that everyone refrain from denouncing the civil and peaceful expression of perspectives that do not align with their own.

- "A healthy tension" refers to a dynamic balance or constructive conflict between different ideas, perspectives, or values. It implies that there can be a productive interplay between opposing viewpoints or forces that leads to better outcomes, growth, and progress – a *tension*, not a *conflict*. This concept acknowledges that a certain level of tension or disagreement can be beneficial in fostering critical thinking, innovation, and the exploration of new ideas.
- In the context of private beliefs and public tolerance in public education and the public sphere in general, maintaining a healthy tension is crucial. On one hand, individuals have the right to hold their personal beliefs, values, and opinions, which can shape their worldview and guide their actions. These private beliefs can be deeply ingrained and influenced by cultural, religious, or philosophical convictions. For many people some private, personal convictions feel non-negotiable.
- The good news is that virtually everyone navigates the private belief-public tolerance tension with great frequency and ease. There are innumerable contexts, from supermarkets to bowling alleys, and from amusement parks to voting centers, in which we uphold the

convention of respecting those with whom we share a space and avoiding confrontation based on differing private beliefs. Doing so is essential in upholding social cohesion and ensuring that public spaces remain welcoming and inclusive to all individuals, regardless of their backgrounds. It reflects a collective understanding that people have the right to hold their personal convictions without fear of judgment or aggression in everyday interactions.

- Public education and other public spheres aim to create inclusive and diverse environments that respect the right to have different perspectives and identities. They strive to promote tolerance, understanding, and the equitable treatment of all individuals, regardless of their backgrounds or beliefs. This commitment to public tolerance ensures that people are not marginalized or discriminated against based on their private beliefs.
- We recognize that in a diverse community, there will be a diversity of views and preferences regarding educational content and methods. We strive to be transparent, clear, and timely in sharing information about all aspects of our educational program, and we regret the inevitability that some elements will not align perfectly with every parent's preference. Accommodating the preferences of every parent regarding what to teach and how to teach it is impossible.
- It is essential for parents whose values, worldviews, ideologies, or beliefs lead them to object to education that includes nonpartisan factual information about the wide range of human social identity diversity and expression to understand that educating children about social identity diversity does not mean promoting any particular ideology or worldview. Rather, it is about providing accurate and factual information to help children understand and appreciate the differences and similarities between people. By teaching children about diversity and how to be respectful towards others, we are helping them become better global citizens who can interact with people from different backgrounds and cultures; we are not telling them what their personal beliefs should be.

Questions/Concerns #7: Equality of Outcomes Requires Dumbing Down Expectations and Disadvantaging Advanced Students

Response

Equity is not about equal outcomes. Equity, the "E" in DEI, is sometimes defined as creating conditions (providing support, accommodation, etc.) that will assure *equality of outcomes*. Whether this definition of equity is conveyed

Reconciling Issues Toward Positive Parent-School Partnership ◆ 65

in the media, promoted by those dedicated to thwarting efforts to increase inclusivity, or misguidedly embraced by DEI practitioners themselves, it is wrong and must be corrected.

Equity seeks to ensure fairness in treatment and opportunities, but equal treatment and opportunities cannot guarantee equal outcomes. As illustrated in the top half of the image below, treating everyone who wants the opportunity to take a bike ride equally by giving them all the same kind of bicycle does not result in equality of opportunity. In fact, it can compromise or even deny the opportunity for some.[1]

The bottom half of the image depicts equity. Each person is provided with a bike that allows them to participate in the bike ride. Equal opportunity is achieved by the unequal provision of types of bikes. The riders are given equal access to the bike they need, not a bike that is good for one lucky or privileged rider. It's important to note that equity, in the form of getting a bike that allows them to take part in the ride, does not guarantee equal outcomes. Getting a suitable bike allows everybody to be included, but it does not guarantee how each rider will do after that.

An elevator as well as stairs in a building gives everyone a chance to reach every floor in the building. It does not determine what any person will want to do, choose to do, or be successful at doing after that. Scissors made for people who are left-handed do not guarantee that the left-handed person will cut as cleanly and creatively as the right-handed person. And golf clubs sized perfectly for you, while putting you on par equity-wise

Figure 1.2 Robert Wood Johnson Equality-Equity image

with other golfers who have the best sized clubs for them, will not automatically result in being on or under par on the links. Equity is about equal access, not equal success.

It's important to take into account that equity at the individual level (e.g., providing a suitable bike to each person) can be insufficient to achieve equality of opportunity. For example, if some people live in areas where road conditions are not safe for biking, having a suitably sized bike would be insufficient to achieving equality of opportunity. Likewise, arriving at a golf club with tailor-fitted clubs only to be confronted by refusal to use the course because of one's racialization or gender will not be enough to bring about equality of access.

Questions/Concerns #8: Parents Should Be Able to Opt Out of Education about Gender and Sexual Orientation Identity Because It Amounts to Sex/Sexuality Education, and Parents Have Rights to Opt Out of Sex/Sexuality Education

Response
Education about gender or sexual orientation identity is not education about sex/sexuality: Just as learning about different foods is not the same as learning how to cook, so education about identity and education about sex are distinct learning areas.

Education about identity encompasses a broad range of topics related to personal and social identities, including but not limited to gender identity and sexual orientation. It aims to promote understanding, empathy, and respect for diverse identities and experiences. Key aspects of education about identity may include the following:

- Learning that some people are naturally drawn to people of the same sex, opposite sex, both, or neither
- Learning that some children have same-sex parents
- Learning that some people do not identify according to the cisgender binary
- Learning that a person's appearance does not necessarily indicate their gender identity
- Learning that there are no scientifically valid reasons to judge people with non-binary or non-heterosexual identities as inferior in any way to people with binary or heterosexual identities

Education about sex (sexual education or sexuality education) focuses specifically on providing information and knowledge about human sexuality, reproductive health, sexual relationships, and sexual behaviors. It aims to equip individuals with accurate and age-appropriate information to support their physical and emotional well-being. Key aspects of education about sex may include the following:

- Biological, genetic, physiological, and anatomical aspects of sex
- Laws governing sexual conduct and consent practices
- Understanding and managing sexual relationship dynamics
- Understanding and making informed reproduction choices

It's crucial to note that discussions about gender identity and sexual orientation within education about identity do not necessarily equate to explicit discussions about sexual acts or behaviors. Education about identity can focus on fostering understanding, respect, and acceptance of diverse identities, while education about sex can provide specific information related to reproductive health, sexual behaviors, and healthy sexual relationships. The first category of education is required for all students in order to support them in avoiding harmful conduct.

It is quite possible to address issues related to gender and sexual orientation separate from explicit discussions about sexual acts or behaviors. Educators and curriculum developers strive to ensure that age-appropriate information is provided, taking into account the developmental stage and needs of students.

Questions/Concerns #9: Placing Kids into So-Called "Affinity Groups" Is Divisive

Response
Crucial Considerations regarding Affinity Groups at Elementary Schools

The "affinity group" model of providing support for underrepresented students is widely practiced in schools across all developmental levels, but this model raises important questions that should be clearly addressed before any school initiates the practice. In recent years, some otherwise well-regarded independent elementary schools have had to weather unflattering public exposure[2] of internal rifts over how affinity groups were conceived, conducted, and communicated.

Beyond knee-jerk resistance and objection based on problematic appeals to colorblindness and/or the conflation of fairness with equity ("If there's one for that group, why isn't there one for my group?" – even when "my group" is a privileged/advantaged group), there are reasonable questions that should be acknowledged and answered before any K–12 school institutes an affinity group. The questions below are specific to affinity groups for *people of color* (a term itself that requires unpacking and specification[3]), but they are applicable to any social identity that might be under consideration for an affinity group (e.g., gender, sexual orientation, class, religion, etc.).

Affinity Group or Identity Group?

What is referred to as *affinity* groups are almost always actually *common identity* groups. Definitionally, *affinity* is about feeling in agreement with and inclined to support or participate in a shared an interest, whatever the interest might be. One might have an affinity for a kind of music, for a certain musician, for a social cause – and not being a musician or a member of the group that might benefit most directly from the social cause need not be a barrier to participation. In other words, technically speaking, affinity is about what and who we *identify with*, not about what we *identify as*. The prevailing model of affinity groups are predicated on a categorical sameness – on the assumption that people who share a sense of same social identity share an identity essence and/or a unique set of experiences, the discussion of which benefits from or even requires separation from people who do not share that same sense of social identity and that same set of unique experiences.

Developmental Factors
- How do affinity groups for children, particularly for our youngest learners, differ from those for adults, and how should developmental differences factor into our decision-making about affinity groups?
- How should a young learner's developing sense of social identity and understanding of social bias and social justice inform approaches to affinity groups?
- How do we avoid projecting or imposing adult perspectives (personal, political, generational) and prescriptions regarding social identity on children whose range and quality of experience with social identity may be similar in some ways to those of adults but are also bound to be significantly different?

Necessary and Sufficient?
- Is the deliberate segregation by racialization required for younger learners to feel sufficient safety and support to express themselves and engage authentically and beneficially in groups designed to support healthful self-regard regarding identity?
- In other words, is an exclusive affinity group the only or best vehicle to the destination we have in mind?
- What does the most advanced and well-grounded literature say about this, and does your school take its cues from that literature?

Eligibility
- How is eligibility determined? Is the group for a narrowly and strictly defined social identity group (e.g., exclusively for black-identified students or black-identified boys or all non-white students)?

The Excluded Students
- What, if anything, is provided for students who are not eligible for the group?
- Especially with younger learners who have not had time and opportunities to learn about the historical of present-day reasons for affinity groups, how does the school mitigate against feelings of confusion, exclusion, alienation, guilt, and possibly resentment?
- Should your school consider a complementary group for white-identified students?
- Does your school have affinity groups for other social identity groups? Should it?
- Does your school have groups for students who share a social identity group interest but not necessarily the "identity" (e.g., Gay-Straight Alliance)? Should it?

Goals and Approach
- What are the explicit goals of the affinity group, and how is success measured?
- What is the frequency, length, and duration of the meetings?
- What is the format and approach – testimonial, topical, instructional, mutual aid, social/recreational?

Intersectionality
- How is the unavoidable fact of the multidimensionality and constant confluence of identities addressed? Must students who identify as members of more than one social identity group (e.g., black-identified, Hispanic-identified, gender-fluid, and neuro-non-majority) choose which of their identities to focus on, or can there be a space in which intersectionality or confluence of salient identities can be explored, discussed, and supported?

Facilitation
- Who facilitates the group?
- How important is providing a mirror of representation for the students?

- Is it OK for a facilitator to be of a different social identity from those participating in the groups? Should that be seen as undermining the safe-space goal?

Communication
- How is the affinity group described to students, families, staff, and the public?

Collaborating with Families
- How are adult family members equipped to support the work happening in the affinity group – including addressing affinity groups that adults might desire (which would set in motion this process of crucial considerations for that constituency)?

To Affinity and Beyond?
- Will the benefits of the affinity groups include creating inclusive bridges or coalitions or even just strategies for group members to feel more empowered and included in the broader community?

The Ultimate Goal
- How are the concerns that catalyzed the desire and decision to provide the group (e.g., achievement gap, defamation, exclusion, etc.) addressed in the school community – with the goal of reducing or eliminating those factors so that the affinity group might not be necessary?

Schools should recognize the steps, cautions, and concerns outlined here when considering common social identity affinity groups. Doing so will assure that any disposition adopted by a school will have been arrived at thoughtfully.

Questions/Concerns #10: How Is It Fair That Some Identities and Cultures Are Celebrated at School and Others Ignored?

Response
Nonpartisan approach to cultural heritages and ideology diversity: Educational communities that aspire to be welcoming of the wide range of social identities among human groups and individuals must do all they can to create a safe and tolerant environment for students, teachers, and parents, while also avoiding promoting or privileging any particular heritage or ideology over another. The goal of striking a balance between education and respect

for differing beliefs and identities is a crucial aspect of maintaining a positive and inclusive school environment.

For schools to be thorough in this area of education and care, it is important to observe a distinction between learning about the great diversity of customs, observances, and occasions held as sacred or otherwise significant to different peoples, cultures, religions, and ethnicities and inducting students into actually observing or celebrating them. School should be where we learn about cultural heritages and ideologies. Home is where we should observe, practice, or celebrate cultural heritages and ideologies.

Schools can and should be places where time is set aside for community-building and celebration. Every school seeks to foster and maintain a sense of community characterized by shared school values, pride in school identity, and opportunities to express the exuberance and joy that are part of being children or teenagers. Luckily, there are ways to approach community building and celebration without relying on programs that represent the privileging of some cultures, heritages, or religions over others.

Next is a letter explaining a shift towards an optimally inclusive approach to heritage holidays at Our School.

_____
_____
_____

Our School's Approach to Heritage Observances
School is for learning about the great diversity of human cultural beliefs and activities; home is for participating in specific heritage beliefs, holidays, and activities.

Dear Our School Parents and Guardians,

I trust this message finds you well. Today, I wish to discuss a delicate yet important topic – our school's approach to cultural observances.

Our School has always been a place where learning thrives, not just academically but socially and culturally. We've celebrated a variety of holidays with enthusiasm, understanding that these moments bring joy and a sense of belonging to many. However, as a diverse educational community, we must be vigilant in ensuring that our celebrations do not inadvertently exclude any member of our school community.

We have traditionally observed holidays like Halloween, Christmas, Hanukkah, Kwanza, Lunar New Year, and Diwali, among others. Such celebrations clearly provide comfort and familiarity to many, yet they carry the risk of excluding others who do not share the same traditions.

As we continue to learn and grow, we find that tradition, while valuable, should not be a static force. Tradition deserves a voice in our conversations, but inclusivity must hold the veto power. It is perfectly understandable to cherish our traditions, yet we must also be willing to evolve our practices to embrace every member of our community.

This is why we are adjusting our approach. Our goal must be to establish new traditions that honor the spirit of celebration and learning without inadvertently privileging or excluding any particular ethnic, cultural, or religious heritage.

One such initiative involves utilizing the ADL Calendar of Observances[4] as a foundation for educational exploration and presentation. This calendar lists a wide array of cultural and religious events from around the world, providing a perfect starting point for our students to engage in learning about the myriad ways the human family celebrates its heritage. After taking a look at the amazing range of heritage occasions observed around the world featured at the ADL site, imagine a digital display in our school's lobby that would show which observances are happening each day. This would provide a constant stream of knowledge about the many ways the vast and diverse human family gathers to reflect, connect, and celebrate important beliefs, values, and traditions.

Further, imagine a project where students collaborate to research and create presentations on holidays and observances from various cultures. This activity would culminate in a "Global Cultural Observations Learning Festival," where students can share their projects, celebrate the diversity of human traditions, and engage with the stories and practices that enrich our global community. Through this, we are not merely learning about but learning from the diversity that surrounds us.

This approach offers a multifaceted learning experience, bringing to life the beauty of our differences while underscoring what unites us. It supports our educational mission to foster a well-rounded understanding of the world, encourage empathy, and cultivate a sense of global citizenship among our students.

The essence of days like Halloween, with its themes of creativity, community, and the joy of dressing up and parading, could be preserved and transformed into events such as "Be the Our School Mascot Day," where students can express their creativity in mascot costume design flair and school spirit in a manner inclusive of all.

In this spirit of inclusivity, we will ensure that no student feels like an outsider during any school event. We will focus on universal themes of joy, kindness, and the shared human experience that draw from various traditions but do not single out any one for exclusive recognition.

I invite you to dialogue with us, share your thoughts, and join us in creating a school environment that respects and honors the diversity that each family brings to our community. We are committed to making Our School a place where every student feels a full and equal member of the school community, regardless of their cultural or religious background.

Your partnership is crucial in this journey, and we value your input. Let us together build a legacy of inclusivity that stands as the hallmark of our school.

Your Truly,

Principal, Our School

Questions/Concerns #11: What if I Simply Can't Abide Some DEI Practices at Our School That I Feel Disrespect and Defy My Right to Say What My Child Will and Will Not Be Exposed To?

Response
When reconciliation is not possible, inclusivity cannot be inclusive of exclusivity

- Acknowledging and respecting diverse viewpoints, engaging in constructive dialogue, and seeking solutions that uphold the principles of inclusivity while respecting individual beliefs can create educational environments that foster understanding, respect, and a sense of belonging for as many stakeholders as possible.
- It is important to acknowledge, however, that viewpoint diversity regarding DEI education can, for some people, result in irreconcilable divergence. If, for example, one holds the belief that there are only two genders, then the idea of teaching their children that there are more than two genders can feel untenable and intolerable. Similarly, if one holds a conviction that homosexuality is not a legitimate sexual orientation, the idea of one's kids being taught about all kinds of families and that there is no evidence to support concern about non-heterosexual orientations might feel offensive.
- Such exclusive stances would be in direct conflict with the requirement to welcome non-cisgender and non-heterosexual students and families and to provide education that fosters respect and tolerance for everyone. Since such a parent preference cannot supersede

anti-discrimination requirements, the prospect of achieving a healthy tension between private belief and public tolerance might be unrealizable. In such a case, the tension is actually a schism, an irreconcilable conflict.

- It is one thing, a terrible thing, to judge someone inferior based on their perceived or avowed identification with a given social identity. Our world is wracked by forms of such bias and bigotry – in the form of racism, sexism, xenophobia, etc. But to regard someone as if an aspect of their being is not only inferior but actually exterior to real and legitimate human characteristics adds obliteration to oppression. *It's not just that the kind of human you are justifies my mistreatment of you; the kind of human you claim to be does not exist.* While this might be a view that someone holds privately, it represents a form of intolerance that cannot be tolerated in an inclusive environment.
- Parents who perceive their disagreement with inclusive education as irreconcilable may choose to seek an alternative educational setting that aligns more closely with their beliefs. Such a decision would represent a parent's prerogative to provide an educational environment that caters to their nonnegotiable convictions and preferences.
- Public schools have to be for everyone, but everyone does not have to choose to educate their child in a public-school setting.

Chapter 3 Summary

Chapter 3 delves into the complexities of parent-school interactions in the context of DEI education. It identifies the skepticism some parents feel towards DEI and offers a pathway to constructive engagement by transparently addressing and demystifying DEI goals and methodologies.

Reframing "parents' rights" from a divisive slogan to an inclusive concept, the chapter affirms every parent's desire for their child's quality education. A hypothetical letter from "Our School" outlines the school's commitment to academic excellence, positioned alongside the indispensable role of DEI initiatives in cultivating a nurturing educational environment.

The chapter critically examines and responds to 11 common parental concerns, aiming to establish a dialogue based on mutual respect and common educational aspirations. Through these discussions, the chapter promotes understanding, counters misunderstandings, and emphasizes legal and moral imperatives for inclusive education, advocating for equitable practices as the cornerstone of a fair learning community.

Reflection and Praxis Prompts

Reflection Prompts

1. Consider a time when a cultural or heritage observance at school made you feel included or excluded. Reflect on how that experience shaped your perspective on school celebrations.
2. Think about "affinity groups" in schools. How might they be beneficial, and what are potential pitfalls that educators should avoid?
3. Recall an instance where you encountered the tension between personal beliefs and public tolerance. How was it navigated, and what was the outcome?
4. Discuss how education about identity can be differentiated from education about sex/sexuality. What are the key distinctions, and why are they important?
5. Reflect on the concept of equity not being about equal outcomes. How does this change your understanding of DEI initiatives in schools?

Praxis Prompts

1. If a parent of one of your students had concerns about DEI practices, how might you engage in a constructive conversation with educators and administrators?
2. Consider the statement: "Inclusivity cannot be inclusive of exclusivity." Discuss the implications of this statement on the ability of schools to cater to all students' needs.

Notes

1 Barlow, J. (2017). Visualizing health equity. *Robert Wood Johnson Foundation*. Retrieved from https://www.rwjf.org/en/insights/our-research/infographics/visualizing-health-equity.html
2 Miller, L. (2015). Can racism be stopped in the third grade? *New York Magazine*. Retrieved June 21, 2015, from https://www.thecut.com/2015/05/can-fieldston-un-teach-racism.html
3 Moses, Y. (2016, December 7). Is the term 'People of Color' acceptable in this day and age? *Sapiens.org*. Retrieved March 3, 2020, from https://www.sapiens.org/language/people-of-color/
4 Anti-Defamation League. (2023). *ADL Calendar of Observances 2024*. Retrieved June 17, 2024, from https://www.adl.org/resources/tools-and-strategies/calendar-observances

4

DEI Integrity

Chapter 4 Quick Capture

DEI leadership in an educational setting is distinguished by its specific focus on fostering a learning environment where diversity is valued, equity is sought, and inclusivity is practiced. DEI leaders must think about how to cultivate a sense of belonging for all students, employees, and families, actively work to dismantle systemic/structural/institutional inequities, and ensure that diversity is pursued, achieved, and sustained without being divisive.

What DEI Leaders Think About:

- ★ Strategic Vision: Crafting a long-term strategy for DEI that aligns with the school's mission and values.
- ★ Current DEI Landscape: Assessing the current state of DEI within the school and identifying areas for improvement.
- ★ Cultural Competency: Building cultural competency and humility within themselves and the school community.

What DEI Leaders Keep Track of:

- ★ Progress and Impact: Monitoring the progress of DEI initiatives and their impact on the school community.

> - ★ Policy Changes: Keeping abreast of changes in legislation and educational policy that affect DEI.
> - ★ Community Feedback: Collecting and responding to feedback from students, parents, and staff on DEI matters.
>
> What DEI Leaders Advocate for:
>
> - ★ Resource Allocation: Advocating for resources that support DEI efforts, such as training programs and diverse hiring practices.
> - ★ Curriculum Inclusivity: Promoting an inclusive curriculum that reflects diverse perspectives.
> - ★ Safe Environments: Ensuring that the school is a safe space for marginalized groups.
>
> What DEI Leaders Need:
>
> - ★ Support from Governance: Endorsement from the board, administration, and supervisors to implement DEI initiatives effectively.
> - ★ Collaboration: A cooperative relationship with all colleagues to engage in and advance DEI work.
> - ★ Open Communication: Clear lines of communication with students and parents to explain the value and objectives of DEI efforts.
> - ★ Protection: Mechanisms to protect them from backlash, such as clear policies against harassment and discrimination.

The Evolution of DEI Leadership

DEI Leadership Since Time Immemorial

The essence of what we now call DEI leadership has indeed always been present in social systems. The roles and responsibilities associated with DEI may have only recently been formalized and given specific titles, but the foundational tasks of ensuring fair inclusion and equitable treatment within a community or organization have historical roots. Before the term "DEI" was coined and formalized, individuals in leadership positions naturally played a role in determining who was included in various societal or organizational groups and how equitably and inclusively members were treated. Throughout history, leaders, whether they be tribal elders, monarchs, religious heads, or community leaders, have had to grapple with issues of who belongs to their communities, how resources are distributed, and how to integrate the diverse elements of their populations.

The principles underlying what we now call DEI leadership have long been a part of social systems and organizational structures throughout history. Thus, DEI work can be seen as an evolution of these ancient responsibilities, modernized to address contemporary understandings of human rights, individual identity, and social justice. While the term DEI might be new, the underlying concepts of inclusion and equity are not. Leaders have always had the power to either maintain the status quo or challenge it to become more inclusive and fairer.

The formalization of DEI roles has given a new shape to these age-old responsibilities, providing a dedicated focus that ensures these critical elements are not an afterthought but are embedded into the core values and operational strategies of modern organizations and societies. This includes schools, corporations, and governments, all of which are now more accountable for their actions and policies regarding diversity, equity, and inclusion.

Recognizing this continuity doesn't diminish the importance of DEI leadership today; rather, it situates it within a long tradition of social governance, emphasizing its fundamental role in shaping fair, inclusive, and prosperous communities.

Historically, leaders from tribal chieftains to monarchs, religious leaders, and heads of state have had the power to include or exclude people based on various criteria, which has impacted the equity and inclusion of different groups. In many cases, these decisions were based on lineage, faith, class, or perceived loyalty. This form of inclusion and exclusion has had lasting impacts, forming the early bedrock of social hierarchies and power dynamics.

With the evolution of modern societies and the development of democratic principles, the criteria and mechanisms for inclusion and equity began to change. DEI aspirations and practices became more expansive, aiming to create more equitable and just societies. Over time, this has led to the emergence of formal roles dedicated to ensuring diversity, equity, and inclusivity within institutions – a recognition that inclusive practices need intentional strategies and leadership to address systemic inequities and foster an environment where all individuals have the opportunity to thrive.

In the contemporary context, DEI leaders draw from a long lineage of decision-making about community membership and resource allocation, but with a new focus on challenging and dismantling historical injustices and systemic biases to create more equitable and inclusive environments. The aim now is not just to make decisions about inclusion but to actively work towards dismantling barriers that have historically prevented full participation in social, educational, and economic systems.

> Starting from the civil rights movements of the 1950s and '60s, which primarily demanded equal rights for individuals based on race and later expanded to include gender, the journey toward recognizing and formalizing DEI roles in organizations has gradually embraced a broader spectrum of social identities, including ethnicity, sexual orientation, and ability.

During the civil rights era, efforts focused on challenging segregation and discrimination, leading to significant legislation such as the Civil Rights Act of 1964 and the Voting Rights Act of 1965. The 1960s also saw the introduction of affirmative action policies aimed at improving opportunities for historically excluded groups.

In subsequent decades, various legislative acts were introduced to protect individuals from discrimination and harassment in the workplace. The establishment of the Equal Employment Opportunity Commission (EEOC) and later laws like the Americans with Disabilities Act (ADA) in 1990.

In educational settings, measures such as the IDEA, originally passed in 1975, and the Title IX amendment of 1972 represent efforts to improve equity and protection for marginalized groups.

The roles specifically dedicated to DEI began to emerge more formally in the late twentieth and early twenty-first centuries as organizations started to recognize the business and social imperatives of a diverse and inclusive workforce. Such roles often started within the human resources departments but gradually became more specialized, reflecting an understanding that DEI concerns are not only about compliance but also about fostering a culture of belonging and respect for all.

Today, DEI leaders play a critical role in driving organizational change by creating strategies to recruit and retain a diverse workforce, designing training programs, and ensuring equitable systems within organizations of all kinds. They are advocates and strategic thinkers who must navigate a complex landscape of social dynamics and organizational/institutional goals and cultures, which sometimes can be at odds with mission-driven DEI-expansionist commitments.

While the DEI field has seen significant progress, it is still evolving, with ongoing discussions about the best practices for integrating these values into every aspect of organizational life, including schools, corporations, and public institutions. The emergence of roles dedicated to DEI-expansivism versus DEI-restrictivism has been met with varying degrees of acceptance, with some recognizing them as essential for social progress and others resisting them out of fear of losing social advantages inherent in historic and current identitarian structures and systems. However, the continuous development and refinement of DEI practices in response to societal changes suggest that these roles are now a fundamental component of modern organizational structures.

Talking the Talk: What Gets Said about DEI

The Pew Research report "School District Mission Statements Highlight a Partisan Divide Over Diversity Equity and Inclusion in K–12 Education" by Meltem Odabaş and Carolina Aragão, dated April 4, 2023,[1] examines the inclusion of diversity, equity, and inclusion (DEI) topics in school district mission statements across the United States. It finds that while mission statements commonly emphasize preparing students for their futures, including goals such as college and job readiness, there is significant variation in the mention of DEI efforts.

According to the analysis of 1,314 mission statements, 34 percent highlight the importance of DEI. This inclusion is more common in Democratic-voting districts, where 56 percent of districts mention DEI, compared to 26 percent in Republican-voting districts. Urban and suburban school districts are more likely to mention DEI than rural ones, with the topic also more common in districts with higher median incomes and a lower proportion of White residents.

The language in mission statements varies greatly, with some of the most common terms being "culture," "diversity," "equity," and "inclusion." Direct mentions of race or nationality are less common. The use of these terms also varies depending on the district's geographic location and the political leanings of its residents.

The report also touches on how terms related to social and emotional learning, future readiness, and safety and health are incorporated into these mission statements. It points out that while a significant number of statements mention providing a safe environment and parental involvement, only a small percentage explicitly mention improving students' mental health as a core educational function.

The findings suggest that school district mission statements serve as a reflection of both educational priorities and the broader political and demographic context of their communities. Common elements of DEI statements in K–12 education, especially as part of a school's mission or standalone statements, include affirmations of a school's commitment to creating a diverse, equitable, and inclusive environment. These statements generally acknowledge the value of a varied community, outline the educational benefits of such diversity, and emphasize the school's role in fostering an inclusive atmosphere where every student has the opportunity to succeed.

The statements also tend to address the need for active engagement in DEI efforts, which might involve curriculum development, extracurricular activities, and community interactions that promote an understanding and appreciation of diversity. Schools may describe specific goals, such as recruiting a diverse staff and student body, developing cultural competency training, and evaluating policies to ensure they support equitable treatment of all students.

In terms of addressing potential challenges and barriers, DEI statements often recognize that bias, discrimination, and underrepresentation exist and outline strategies to address these issues, which can include revising recruitment and retention policies, promoting professional development, and ensuring equitable access to resources and opportunities.

Furthermore, many DEI statements recognize the need for ongoing reflection and action, implying that DEI work is iterative and needs consistent attention and adaptation as the school community evolves and new challenges emerge.

DEI statements are living documents that reflect the ongoing commitment of an educational community to respond to and grow with the needs of its diverse population. They serve as guiding principles for policy-making, teaching, and learning within the institution. That schools vary in how they address DEI in their statements should not lead us to conclude that some schools are more engaged in DEI than others. As explained in Chapter 1, there is no human dynamic in which diversity, equity, and inclusivity are not inextricably inherent. Every school, and in fact every human collective, would do well to explicitly articulate how it approaches its DEI dynamics.

Walking the Walk: The Discrepancies and Dissonance That Often Exist Between a School's Professed DEI Goals and the Reality of Its Practices and Policies

Integrity as psychological wholeness refers to an individual's sense of being complete or whole within themselves. This involves acknowledging, accepting, and integrating the various parts of one's identity and experiences. It's about having a self-concept that is cohesive and stable, where different aspects of the self are in harmony. Psychological integration allows individuals to feel authentic and true to themselves, which is essential for good mental health and well-being. When this sense of wholeness is compromised, an individual may experience disintegration, which can manifest as internal conflict, confusion, and distress over one's sense of self.

Integrity in terms of convictions and values relates to consistently acting in ways that are congruent with one's ethical beliefs and principles. This form of integrity is often associated with moral uprightness, honesty, and fairness. It requires self-awareness, principled decision-making, and the courage to stand by one's beliefs, even in the face of personal cost or external pressure. Integration, in this context, would be the alignment between one's actions and beliefs, leading to a reputation for trustworthiness and ethical behavior. Disintegration occurs when there's a breach between what one professes to value and how one actually behaves, which can lead to a sense of hypocrisy, guilt, or shame.

Both forms of integrity are vital for personal development and for maintaining trust and respect in interpersonal relationships. They are foundational to leadership, as leaders are expected to model both psychological integrity and moral integrity, creating environments where others feel valued and inspired to also act with integrity.

When DEI Leadership Is Strong and Empowered

In 2020, in the throes of the perfect storm of the Covid pandemic, the murder of George Floyd, and the Trump presidency, a middle school recognized the need for students to have safe, structured, non-partisan opportunities to gain accurate, factual information and explore and exchange views on the confluence of intense physical health, mental health, social justice, and political dynamics roiling in America and across the globe. In response, the school went above and beyond customary DEI efforts such as clubs and celebrations, and created a course for sixth-, seventh-, and eighth-graders.

The course met weekly for one term. The course was a seminar model that featured ways for students to provide their input into what would be explored from session to session, clear guidelines to ensure constructive and candid participation, and trust in students to rise about the divided and divisive rancor surrounding them in society. The adult facilitators of the seminar sections were faculty volunteers, well-versed in providing guidance on topics related to social identity, social bias, and social justice. This team of facilitators met regularly to share impressions, respond to emergent needs, and support each other (after all, they too were surrounded by rampant societal discord).

Every week, as part of a weekly collection of notes to parents submitted by every sixth-, seventh-, and eighth-grade teacher of every subject taught in those grades, a Seminar note was included. It explained what was covered, why and how it was covered, and how the students were doing navigating the content and their interactions with each other. Every entry ended with full-throated encouragement for parents to check in with their child about the week's session and contact their child's facilitator and/or the course coordinator with questions or concerns. Many parents sent notes of appreciation. Not one parent expressed a concern or complaint.

The following is the session plan for a midterm meeting. It features a review and discussion of student feedback and input on "The topics I most hope we cover," "How I hope we can approach our learning and discussions to keep them safe, engaging, and useful," and "My sense of safety, comfort, and welcome in the seminar." As you can see, the students were eager to explore a wide range of topics related to diversity, equity, and inclusivity, had clear ideas and intentions about how to create and maintain a space that was safe enough for them to be brave enough to say what they needed to say, and they were successful in doing so.

How the Seminar Exemplified What a DEI Leader Must Think About, Keep Track of, Advocate for, and Needs in Order to Fulfil Their Role

What DEI Leaders Must Think About

Strategic Vision: DEI leaders must think about how attention to diversity, equity, and inclusivity is integral to realizing a school's mission and upholding a school's values. The development and provision of the seminar in response to students' need for clear information and a safe space within which to exchange and synthesize perspectives was a shining example of living the mission, vision, and values of a school that is clear about its commitment to pursuing academic excellence and honoring differences.

Current DEI Landscape: DEI leaders must constantly assess the current state of DEI within the school, identify areas for improvement, and work to mobilize the community toward the common goal of optimal inclusivity. The DEI seminar arose from the recognition that the school's sense of community was under the strain of societal dissonances that could not be kept outside of the school building and needed to be carefully and constructively addressed in safe and age-appropriate ways.

Antibias Capacity: DEI leaders must seek and provide ways to build antibias skills within themselves and the school community. Developing the DEI seminar for middle schoolers required making sure seminar facilitators and all teachers were ready to engage with issues of the day and students who were mightily trying to make sense of it all. That required creating a safe space for facilitators and all staff to get their own bearing on the dynamics and tensions and be good models of civil, non-partisan discussion.

What DEI Leaders Must Keep Track Of

Progress and Impact: Monitoring the progress of DEI initiatives and their impact on the school community. DEI leaders must not merely develop and provide promising programs and rely on impression or anecdote as a means of verifying efficacy. Data, whether qualitative, quantitative, or both must be collected and brought to bear on the question of efficacy. The feedback from students regarding their sense of safety in the seminar provided data on the impact of the program.

I. The topics I most hope we cover going forward – ranked, with #1 being most important to me

Rank 1	Rank 2	Rank 3	Rank 4 & beyond
• Gender discrimination (in general) • Anti-Semitism • Social Identity Pyramid • Black Lives Matter • BLM and the protests • BLM and ALM • Black Lives Matter, Blue Lives Matter, All Lives Matter • Racial discrimination in other countries and what that looked like and how they overcame them • What is implicit bias? • Understanding & applying empathy • Politics • How people are reacting to the election	• Climate change • The pay gap (how much more money men make then women) • Physical appearance • Stereotypes • Stereotypes about woman and their role in society • Discrimination against women/how we can prevent that • Biases & stereotypes against physical appearance, for example, some people think of blond people as dumb, especially blond women • Why do people have discriminations about women? • Social Status	• LGBTQ rights • Disabilities • Recent space advancements • What makes us divide • Learning people's experiences • Nationality • Social identity unearned benefits & biases • Eating disorders • What is personal identity? • Is "race" a choice? Can I choose what race I identify as? • quality and equity • Stereotypes towards Asians and Muslims • Finding your identity	• Ageism • Our community expectations • How history affects us today • Riots vs protests • What it means to be an ally and how to be one? (for anything) • Wealth differences • Native American history • How making these assumptions can hurt people • Racial identity • Immigration • Homosexuality • What is implicit bias? • Heritage

• What's the best way to understand gender and respect a person's gender identity? • Black people's perspective • Sexuality	• If when Joe Biden is inaugurated Trump will make it a violent thing • The president trying to overrule the election • Covid-19's effect of Asian Identified people • Identity • Religion • Abortion laws • How can I be friends with someone who has very different beliefs on topics that are important to me? • Things not in the social prism • Race • Racism • Understanding how people feel	• White supremacy • How we can help support people • Animal rights	• How to be considerate when talking about these types of things, and to have a non-biased opinion, and a considerate one (not that there are people who are doing this) • How to help fight for people's rights

II. **How I hope we can approach our learning and discussions to keep them safe, engaging, and useful**

- Ask questions to get us thinking.
- We can make sure everyone gets to talk, I think in the future, if we go back onsite, the school should try to get an "owl" (a robot that spins so the teacher can see the entire class) because I am in the corner so you aren't able to see me when I raise my hand which can be a problem sometimes.

(*Continued*)

(Continued)

- Maybe do Kahoot or other activities like that so we can be engaged.
- I think all our discussions have been under control. One thing I like about the discussions is everyone has a voice, and your voice is heard.
- I hope that we can let everyone speak, and not judge other people for their thoughts and opinions.
- I think that you did a good job approaching them this semester, but if you could tell people the day before about what we are talking about if the topic is going to be hard, that would be good.
- I hope that we could learn about something and discuss it politely.
- I think we need to be respectful. I think that we need to listen to our classmates and not interrupt. I think that we need to consider what they are saying even if we don't agree.
- I hope that we can make sure to honor and respect people's opinions and make sure everyone is heard if they want to be.
- I hope that everyone can feel like they are included and entitled to their opinion. I hope that everyone knows that even if they don't want to speak, they can.
- I think that if we respect people's opinions and help people think in a different way, it will feel safe.
- Not to make others feel bad about themselves. To keep respecting others' opinions.
- The same how we have before.
- I hope that we use the system we came up with in advisory; if we disagree on something, we take a deep breath and go about disagreeing respectfully.
- Everyone being respectful, but also being able to share their opinions.
- I can approach our learning discussions calmly.
- One way to keep kids more engaged is to interact with the class more often, like ask kids questions and opinions, but safely.
- Starting from facts and making sure everything we say is accurate and we can back it up. Respecting others' opinions is also important, as long as we still know the difference between opinions and facts.

- I THINK WE NEED TO BE KIND AND STAY CALM EVEN WHEN CERTAIN EVENTS ARE REALLY HARD TO TALK ABOUT.
- I hope we can learn things in a way that is educational but also to make sure people are comfortable with it.
- Be respectful.
- Making sure people feel included

III. My sense of safety, comfort, and welcome in the seminar

- I'm good. It's a safe place, comfortable place, and welcome place.
- In a one to ten number scale, I feel like a 10; no one ever says anything to make me not feel comfortable in this learning space.
- I feel safe and haven't encountered a situation where I didn't ever feel safe.
- I feel very comfortable in the seminars even when we talk about some dark and cruel things.
- On a scale from one to ten, it's probably a seven or eight mainly because topics can be sensitive, and you are worried you will word it wrong and offend.
- I feel safe and welcome. I just think that sometimes I think too much about being called on and not enough about the actual question.
- I feel safe saying almost anything.
- I feel comfortable with some topics, but not so comfortable with others.
- 89 out of 100.
- A lot of safety, comfort, and welcome.
- When we're able to have calm discussions, even if two people disagree.
- I FEEL SAFE. I JUST THINK THAT WE NEED TO BE MAYBE A LITTLE MORE EASY ON SCARY EVENTS.
- Eight to ten. I have always felt very comfortable talking and sharing my opinion in class. I think I know everyone on my cohort pretty well, and I am not scared to say anything.
- I feel very safe, welcome, and comfortable in the seminars because everyone respects everyone and listens to everyone else, and if they disagree with my opinion, they will say it politely.
- For sure. I feel safe while talking.

(Continued)

(Continued)

- I never feel too uncomfortable during the seminar.
- I feel okay about it. It's just sometimes hard to focus.
- I think that my safety is welcome in the seminar, most of the time. Sometimes the way they approach certain topics makes it seem like they're partial to one side, which makes me feel unwelcome if I think differently.
- I feel welcome, comfortable, and safe in the seminar.
- I feel very safe; so far no one has been doing many assumptions, everyone's very thoughtful, the teacher is giving thorough explanations and letting people ask lots of questions.
- I feel very welcome in the seminar.
- I have a good sense of safety in the seminar, because I don't feel like I'm being mistreated by anyone in my cohort.

Policy Changes: Keeping abreast of changes in legislation and educational policy that affect DEI. The seminar emerged during the Covid pandemic period, health and safety measures taken to minimize spread of the virus had direct impacts on school policy and students' sense of safety, and brought to the fore issues of equity and social justice regarding risk and access to treatment. The seminar facilitators remained abreast of these changes and impacts, and empowered students to gain relevant information and process their feelings constructively.

Community Feedback: Collecting and responding to feedback from students, parents, and staff on DEI matters. Keeping parents informed about the seminar and soliciting their questions was effective in maintaining parents' confidence that communication about the course was transparent and substantive.

What DEI Leaders Must Advocate For

Resource Allocation: Advocating for resources that support DEI efforts, such as training programs and diverse hiring practices. To create equitable work and compensation dynamics, the seminar facilitators were allowed to step back from some of their duties while providing the seminar experience. Additionally, materials needed for students and facilitators were made available at no cost to them. This responsive provision of necessary resources and workload adjustment was crucial to making the seminar possible.

Curriculum Inclusivity: Promoting an inclusive curriculum that reflects diverse perspectives. The seminar was a clear demonstration of inclusive curriculum focused as it was on inclusivity dynamics in society and designed to foster a sense of safety and belonging for every student who participated.

Safe Environments: Ensuring that the school is a safe space for marginalized groups. Care was taken to make it clear that while many of the topics covered in the seminar centered on how people were treated based on their perceived membership in social identity groups, there was no expectation the exploration and discussion of these topics had to include testimony by students who identified as members of any groups under consideration. We were there to study and understand the issues, not put anyone on the spot to speak for those with whom they might share social identities. It was also made clear that holding different views on topics was a reflection of the diversity in our groups. The seminar was a place to practice civil and constructive discussion of controversial topics – a space in which there might be disagreement at times but never the need for disagreeable manners.

What DEI Leaders Need

Support from Governance: Endorsement from the board, administration, and supervisors to implement DEI initiatives effectively. The school's leadership was unequivocally supportive of the seminar as a needed and valuable opportunity for students to carefully and collaboratively consider important issues of the times.

Collaboration: A cooperative relationship with colleagues who are willing to engage in DEI work. All middle school staff were kept aware of what was being discussed in the seminar and how students were doing so that they could engage with students as indicated beyond the seminar experience. This was important in cases where students might have questions or concerns about topics or aspects of the seminar experience. Being able to talk with a trusted teacher beyond the seminar helped some students deepen their sense of safety and understanding of the issues.

Open Communication: Clear lines of communication with students and parents to explain the value and objectives of DEI efforts. As noted, effective methods to communicate with and solicit feedback from parents and students were in place.

Protection: Mechanisms to protect them from backlash, such as clear policies against harassment and discrimination. Facilitators felt not only protected but encouraged to provide the important service of leading the seminar.

When DEI Leadership Is Disempowered

A DEI leader was approached by a black-identified student via an email in which they conveyed their concern that two students of color had been mistreated by a white-identified administrator that left them feeling targeted based on their racialization. Soon after receiving that note, the DEI leader received an email directly from one of the students who had been mistreated.

The student reported that as she and her friend were getting a snack, one breakfast bar each from the kitchen area as they waited at the end of the school day for the bus that would take them from the suburban school campus to their homes in an urban area, the Associate Head of School (AHS), a person who had worked at the school for over two decades, approached them and asked them why they were stealing.

Taken aback by this accusation, the two students, both seventh-graders, one who had been at the school since kindergarten, the other in her first year, emphatically assured the adult that they were not stealing and in fact had permission from the head of the kitchen to take a snack whenever they were waiting after school for their bus to arrive. A large bowl with assorted granola bars and other such snacks was always out on a table in the dining area for that reason. Accessing it didn't require anything more than walking into the dining area, a large open space, the interior of which was visible to anyone walking by.

Despite the reassurance from the students, the AHS not only did not rescind her allegation but instead asked the students why they were lying. According to the students, at this point they became not only upset and anxious but also angry at how they were being treated. One of them, who had known this adult for years, was particularly distraught to be confronted in this way.

As the students were trying to convince the AHS that they had done nothing wrong, the director of the kitchen came out of the food preparation area behind the dining area. Having heard the tense back-and-forth that was happening between the students and the AHS, the kitchen director came out to affirm the student's account that they did in fact have permission directly from the kitchen director to help themselves to a snack to tide them over between the end of the afterschool program and getting home on any given day.

The two students as well as the director of the kitchen noted later that they were dismayed that at the point that the AHS received a correction of their perception of wrongdoing, they did not simply apologize for their error in judgment. Instead, without further remark, the AHS simply walked away.

After hearing from that student, who was distraught over the experience, the DEI leader spoke with their parents to make sure they were aware of their child's need for support, to learn their perspective on the situation, and to offer support. The parents, both of whom the DEI leader knew from many interactions in many contexts at school, were also distraught, very concerned about their daughter, and deeply hurt that this could have happened at a school they had trusted to treat their child with dignity, respect, and love.

After talking with this student's parents and reaching out to the other student's family, the DEI leader reached out to the AHS to learn their perspective on the matter and support. To the DEI leader's great surprise, the AHS refused to talk to the DEI leader about the situation. They said they would be talking with the Head of School and preferred to not engage with the DEI leader.

Over a period of days during which the students received no resolution of the situation despite letting the DEI leader know that they felt they deserved an apology from the AHS, the AHS not only persisted in refusing to engage with the DEI leader but filed a complaint against them with the human resources officer and the Head of School. During this period, despite their appeal to the HOS to require that the AHS comply with expectations to work with the DEI leader on matters related to social identity, social justice, and social bias, the HOS maintained a reluctance and adopted a stance of wanting to honor the AHS' concerns about what they claimed was a mishandling of the situation by the DEI leader.

After the DEI leader addressed every item of complaint made by the AHS, demonstrating with indisputable clarity that none of them were valid and raising the concern that the AHS's complaint was filed disingenuously and amounted to retaliation for the DEI leader's attempt to simply fulfil their duty to engage in matters related to diversity, equity, and inclusivity, and address concerns brought to them by the students and their families, the head of Human Resources (HR) hastily requested that the DEI leader make themselves available for a meeting with the AHS. According to the HR, the purpose of the meeting would be for the AHS to apologize for their conduct both with the students and toward the DEI leader. It was made explicitly clear in writing that there could be no further discussion during the meeting beyond the AHS's expression of apology.

The apology meeting was scheduled for a Sunday morning at the school, at a time when other people were not present. The DEI leader agreed to attend in hopes that this might be a step forward through the impasse, confusion, and frustration that had marked the period of time since learning about the incident.

To their dismay, the DEI leader found that after receiving what was clearly a carefully scripted apology which had obviously vetted by at least the HR manager from the AHS who had obviously been supported/coached regarding comportment during the meeting, there was no further action on the part of the school to allow the DEI leader to fulfil their role in working with members of the community to prevent, address, and resolve matters related to diversity, equity, and inclusivity. The apology did nothing to acknowledge their disenfranchisement from a process that was at the core of their role and professional integrity.

Ultimately, it became clear to the DEI leader that for reasons they might never know, the school, as represented by the HOS, the HR manager, the AHS, and, it was assumed, any other relevant parties (e.g., board members and legal counsel), could offer nothing beyond allowing them to absorb everything that had happened and carry on in their role. So painful and powerful a blow was this to the DEI leader's sense of integrity, ethics, and professionalism that they tendered their resignation.

These illustrations of what can happen when the essential elements of DEI leadership are addressed and when they are not provide both inspiration and caution which can be used to navigate the terrain of DEI leadership with clarity or purpose, commitment to providing support, and integrity.

Common Obstacles to Optimal DEI Leadership

DEI leadership obstacles to look out for, confront, and eliminate, particularly in K–12 education, are multifaceted and often deeply entrenched in the cultural and operational fabric of institutions. These obstacles can be broadly categorized as follows:

Hierarchical Hurdles: Educational institutions are often steeped in traditional hierarchies that can hinder DEI initiatives. When nominal authority is deferred to over the experience and expertise of DEI professionals, it can undermine the implementation of effective programs and policies. Schools must empower DEI leaders to enact change, even when it challenges long-standing power structures.

Influence of Powerful Constituencies: At times, the preferences and interests of influential community members, such as major donors or prominent families, can take precedence over DEI objectives. This can lead to a misalignment between a school's stated commitment to DEI and its actions.

Unacknowledged Bias: Even the most well-intentioned individuals can have blocked spots (the inability to see past pride or ignorance and acknowledge harmful behavior). Schools often struggle to confront the possibility that their actions or policies, however unintentional, can perpetuate harm or inequality.

Blaming the Messenger: DEI leaders are charged with not only facilitating the celebration of diversity and inclusivity but also calling attention to areas for growth and bringing their experience and skills (e.g., empathic support, conflict resolution, bullying prevention, etc.) to bear in circumstances where conflict or harm associated with social identity, social bias, and social justice occur. It's crucial that substantive information about areas of concern not be seen as products of the DEI leader's personality, agenda, social identity, or simply incorrect assessment.

Accountability Avoidance: Reluctance to hold individuals accountable, particularly those with seniority or close ties to decision-makers, can impede progress. Accountability is crucial for fostering an environment where DEI values are not only preached but practiced.

Lack of Continuity: DEI efforts can falter without consistent leadership and support. The departure of key DEI advocates or changes in administration can disrupt the momentum of DEI programs.

Resistance to Change: Change can be challenging, and some staff, faculty, parents, and governors may resist DEI efforts due to discomfort or disagreement with the principles of equity and inclusivity. It's important for leaders to navigate these waters with sensitivity while also being firm in their commitment to DEI.

Resource Limitations: DEI work requires not only moral support but also tangible resources. Schools often face budgetary constraints that can limit the scope and effectiveness of DEI initiatives.

Measurement Challenges: Assessing the impact of DEI initiatives can be complex. Schools may struggle to develop metrics that accurately reflect progress in creating a more inclusive environment.

Communication Breakdowns: Effective DEI leadership involves transparent and ongoing communication with all stakeholders. Misunderstandings or a lack of clarity around DEI goals and strategies can hinder community buy-in.

Cultural Inertia: Shifting the culture of an institution to be more inclusive requires sustained effort. Traditions and norms may be deeply rooted, and altering them to be more equitable can be met with resistance or apathy.

Chapter 4 Summary

Chapter 4 delves into the crucial aspects of DEI leadership, exploring the various components of what DEI leaders must think about, such as strategic vision and cultural competency; what they must track, including progress, policy changes, and community feedback; what they advocate for, like resource allocation and curriculum inclusivity; and what they need, including support from governance and open communication channels. The chapter articulates that while the term "DEI" may be modern, the essence of its leadership is an age-old concept that has been a part of social systems throughout history, albeit under different guises.

The chapter examines how DEI leaders can navigate and overcome common obstacles in K–12 education, such as hierarchical hurdles, the influence of powerful constituencies, unacknowledged bias, accountability avoidance, and resource limitations. Through a blend of historical context and contemporary analysis, it sheds light on the evolution of DEI leadership from ancient times to its current incarnation. The chapter underscores the importance of consistency and integrity in leadership to maintain trust and effectiveness in promoting DEI values within an institution. Ultimately, "DEI Integrity" challenges educators and leaders to move beyond mere lip service, advocating for a model of DEI leadership that is empowered, dynamic, and responsive to the needs of a diverse school community.

Reflection and Praxis Prompts

Reflection Prompts

1. Reflect on the historical context of DEI leadership mentioned in the chapter. Can you identify moments in history when inclusivity or equity was notably advanced or impeded by leadership decisions?
2. Considering the strategic vision needed for DEI, reflect on a time when a leader's vision impacted inclusivity within an organization.
3. Can you recall times when your leadership was robustly supported and times when it was not? What were the circumstances? How did it feel, and what did you do in each instance?

Praxis Prompts

1. How can leaders assess the current DEI landscape in their schools? What tools or measures could be put in place to gauge progress?
2. Discuss ways in which educators can build antibias skills within their communities. What programs or practices have you observed or can imagine would effectively cultivate these skills?
3. As a leader, how would you advocate for resources to support DEI efforts? Consider both financial and non-financial resources.
4. Curriculum Inclusivity: What strategies can be employed to ensure that a school's curriculum is truly inclusive? How do you address the potential pushback?
5. Safe Environments: Describe a scenario where the school environment did not feel safe for all students. How can DEI leaders work to create safer spaces?
6. Addressing Discrepancies: Reflect on a time when a school's DEI rhetoric did not match its actions. How did it impact the community, and what steps would you take to bridge that gap?

Note

1 Odabas, M., & Arogão, C. (2023, April 4). School district mission statements highlight a partisan divide over diversity equity and inclusion in K–12 education. *Pew Research Center*. Retrieved February 5, 2024, from https://www.pewresearch.org/social-trends/2023/04/04/school-district-mission-statements-highlight-a-partisan-divide-over-diversity-equity-and-inclusion-in-k-12-education/.

PART TWO

Praxis

Touchstones and Tools You Can Use

Tools You Can Use

Providing "tools you can use" in trainings, workshops, or books designed to support educators in understanding and practicing diversity, equity, and inclusivity (DEI) is vital for several reasons. These tools not only enhance the learning experience but also empower and equip educators to implement DEI principles effectively in their professional settings. We hope the provision of these Touchstones and Tools will do the following:

1. Facilitate Application of Concepts

DEI concepts can often seem abstract or theoretical, making it challenging for educators to understand how to apply them in real-world classroom settings. Providing concrete tools and strategies helps translate these abstract concepts into actionable steps. This bridge between theory and practice is essential for educators to feel confident in applying DEI principles in their lesson planning, classroom management, and interactions with students and colleagues.

2. Encourage Active Engagement

Tools such as interactive exercises, reflection prompts, case studies, and practical strategies encourage active engagement with the material. Active engagement enhances learning retention and makes the DEI training more impactful. When educators actively participate in applying what they learn through practical tools, they are more likely to internalize the principles and understand their application.

3. Support Customized Implementation

Every educational environment is unique, with its specific challenges and opportunities related to DEI. Offering a variety of tools allows educators to select and customize approaches that best fit their classroom dynamics, school culture, and community context. This flexibility is crucial for the effective implementation of DEI initiatives, as it considers the diverse needs and backgrounds of students and staff.

4. Promote Continuous Learning and Reflection

DEI is an evolving field. Understanding and implementing its principles requires ongoing learning and reflection. Tools that include reflective questions, self-assessments, and planning templates encourage educators to continually reflect on their practices, biases, and the impact of their actions. This ongoing process of reflection and learning is essential for personal growth and the development of an inclusive educational environment.

DOI: 10.4324/9781003510673-8

5. Build Confidence and Competence

Educators often recognize the importance of DEI but may feel unsure about their ability to address complex issues related to race, gender, sexuality, social advantage and disadvantage, and other issues related to social identity, social bias, and social justice. Practical tools provide educators with a sense of competence and confidence in their ability to navigate these sensitive topics. This empowerment is crucial for fostering an inclusive classroom where all students feel seen, respected, and valued.

6. Facilitate Measurable Progress

Tools that offer structured activities, assessment rubrics, and feedback mechanisms help educators and institutions to measure progress over time. This ability to assess and reflect on the effectiveness of DEI efforts is crucial for continuous improvement and accountability. It also helps in identifying areas for further development and celebrating successes in creating more inclusive educational spaces.

Touchstone/Tool #1: It Begins Immediately; Who Is This Person?

The It Begins Immediately; Who Is This Person? exercise is designed to be an icebreaker that engages participants in a highly interactive mix of connecting with the presenter, collaborating with other participants, and exploring social identity categories in a way that is thought-provoking, group-building, and fun.

Goals
1. To engage participants in fun, connective, collaboration right away
2. To interactively explore how we arrive at impressions about people's identities
3. To accept that making assumptions is part and parcel of being human, and that checking assumptions is crucial to avoiding error and offense in human interactions

Materials
1. The It Begins Immediately; Who Is This Person? worksheet
2. Writing instruments

The It Begins Immediately; Who Is This Person? worksheet
   Please note your first-impression thoughts and speculations about the following aspects of MY identity.

   Sex
   Gender
   Ethnicity
   Culture
   Race
   Age
   Physical Condition (any disabilities?)
   Sexual Orientation
   Spiritual Orientation
   Political Orientation
   Marital Status
   Social Status (socioeconomic, etc.)
   Social Privileges/Advantages
   Social Disadvantages
   Agenda

Procedure

Part One – Instructions
1. Explain to the participants that you'd like to begin the session by telling them a little about yourself, but not in the customary way. Instead of you telling them about you, you'd like them to tell you about you.
2. Hand out the exercise worksheet, and read the name of the exercise: "It Begins Immediately; Who Is This Person?" then explain that you are the person referred to in the title, and their job is to note their impression of you in 15 areas shown on the worksheet.
3. Explain that this is not a test, that you won't be collecting the worksheets, and that they need not and should not spend a lot of time thinking about each item, and instead just note what comes to mind.
4. Explain that soon you will leave the room to allow them to (1) take just a few minutes (two or three at most) to fill in the worksheet and then (2) talk with the folks at their table or next to them to share and compare their results.
5. Let the participants know that you'll be coming back into the rooms after about ten minutes, at which time you ask them what they came up with in each category. Encourage them to try to get to every category!
6. Tell them that before you leave and let them get to work, you'd like to give them a full view of you, then stand still, hold your arms straight to the sides, away from your body, slowly turn around 360 degrees, and then exit the space.

Part Two – Sharing Assumptions
Part Two of the exercise is the opportunity for the participants to experience what it feels like to be given permission to pay attention to the assumptions they are automatically making about another person's identities (in this case, yours), to note them, and to share their assumptions with others. While you're outside of the room, if you stay close enough to hear what's happening in the room, you'll no doubt hear lots of energetic conversation and laughter. This exercise never fails to get people talking and laughing with each other.

Part Three – Exploring Our Assumptions
1. When you re-enter the room, note to the participants how nice it is to hear so much conversation and laughter.
2. Let them know that now it's time for them to tell you about you. Assure them that there is nothing they can say about you in any of

the categories that could hurt your feelings. Perhaps make a joke about having thick skin or about having heard it all already.
3. Begin with the first category, Sex, and proceed from there through each of the categories (or as many as you feel time will allow) by asking two questions consistently: (1) *What is my* [fill in the blank with the category you are on]? and (2) *How do you know?*

> The first question prompts participants to simply say what they noted about you in the given category. Be sure to ask for several responses so that the range of results is noted. If there's unanimity note that. Throughout this part of the exercise, congratulate the participants on being comfortable and/or brave enough to share their impressions.
>
> The second question is where the learning kicks in. It leads participants to explore where their indicators come from and then ask the question: Where do your indicators of what I am in each category come from?
>
> The participants will become focused on the fact that they have a set of cognitive instructions for determining what someone is in every social identity category. For instance, in the case of sex, you will likely hear that they determined you were the sex they landed on because of your body shape, your voice, the way you dress, your name, and other customary indicators of sex identity.
>
> By repeating these two questions for every category, the participants will move into a comfortable rhythm of examining the bases on which they make identity assumptions. Feel encouraged to also ask other relevant questions, such as, "Why do we think there seemed to be reluctance to share impressions about my sexual orientation?" That category tends to lead participants to want to avoid making (or sharing) their assumptions in light of current social vigilance to avoid offense. Consider recognizing that as laudable, and consider wondering with the group why that didn't seem to be the case for other categories.

Part Four – Why This Exercise?

The "Agenda" category is there to prompt the question: "What's my agenda in doing this exercise? Why would I choose to start our work together this way?"

This question directs participants to articulate their own realizations about the power and automaticity of making assumptions about identities. This is a perfect place to affirm that despite common encouragement to not make assumptions, making assumptions is not something we can avoid.

Assumptions have always been necessary for humans to make it through their days and their lives. Here you can provide examples such as assuming there will be a floor on the other side of a closed door you are about to open and walk through. Assumptions are clearly not always bad and clearly not always avoidable. But when it comes to making assumptions about people, since it begins immediately and automatically upon encountering another person and might involve stereotypes and prejudice, we would all do well to always check our assumptions.

Also consider adding to your reasons for starting with the exercise your hope that it leaves them with confidence that your work together can be energetic, interactive, connective, enlightening, and even fun at times, and that you welcome candid, constructive, conversation.

Part Five – The Big Reveal

Before moving on, share how you self-identify in each of the exercise categories.

Touchstone/Tool #2: Willing, Ready, and on Belay

"Willing, Ready, and on Belay" the experience of a ropes course challenge, specifically the Pamper Pole, to metaphorically explore themes of trust, risk-taking, and community support in personal growth and learning environments. It offers a narrative that encapsulates the journey of engaging in challenging situations with the support of others, which is likened to being 'on belay' during a high ropes course.

Goals of Using the Reading
- To facilitate understanding of personal and community roles in facing challenges.
- To underscore the importance of establishing a safe space for open dialogue on sensitive topics.
- To enhance empathy and support within groups, promoting a sense of trust and collective responsibility.
- To create parallels between physical risk-taking and the psychological risks in DEI discussions.

How to Use the Reading
1. *Preparation:*
   - Ensure participants have access to the text of "Willing, Ready, and On Belay." Consider providing it as a "pre-read" to be done before everyone comes together for the program during which it will be discussed.
   - For those unfamiliar with the Pamper Pole activity, please consider finding a video of someone experiencing the Pamper Pole.
   - Set the stage for the discussion by introducing the concept of the Pamper Pole and its relevance to social discourse.
2. *Initial Reading:*
   - Have participants read the text individually or in groups, encouraging them to think about the situations where they've taken risks or supported others.
3. *Discussion Facilitation:*
   - Use the story as a springboard for discussion. Encourage participants to share their interpretations and personal connections to the narrative.
   - Discuss the metaphors used in the text and how they relate to group dynamics, especially in DEI contexts. What constitutes *willingness* to take part, what helps folks feel *ready* for challenges

they might face, and how are supports (*belay*) provided to keep everyone *safe enough to be brave enough* to take part.
4. Practical Application:
- Apply the concepts from the reading to real-life DEI scenarios within the group or community.
- Consider role-play or other interactive activities to embody the support systems discussed in the reading.

Willing, Ready, and On Belay: One Teacher's Approach to Establishing a Safe Space

A long, long time ago, when I stood on sturdier, springier legs, while working at a residential summer camp in bucolic West Poland, Maine, I volunteered to be the first person to try a new element at the camp's brand-new ropes course. The new element was called "The Pamper Pole" (so named for its metaphorical effect of inducing the need for a change of britches following the harrowing experience).

I was a big advocate of the kind of experiential learning that adventure-based programs afforded, and I was fairly comfortable with adventurous physical activity. My investment in this sort of thing combined with my general familiarity and comfort made it easy for me to say "Sure, let's do this!"

Our ropes course specialist provided a clear explanation of the pamper pole experience. He explained that the function of the apparatus – a roughly 30 foot pine tree stripped of its branches and fitted with pegs to be used to climb to a small platform affixed to the top of the pole (roughly 1 foot square) – was to provide a balance-challenging perch from which one was to leap, in an effort to grasp a trapeze that dangled about 8 feet from the pole.

So much for function. What was the *purpose* of this device? Why would anyone want to climb a wobbly pole, stand on a too-small perch, and leap out into thin air to try to grab a bar attached to two ropes? *To dare*; to face fear with courage; to gain the satisfaction of succeeding; to learn to live with disappointment; to imbibe the mix of humility and pride that leads one to try, try again; and to apply the lessons learned to life beyond the literal leap from an actual pole.

In addition to explaining the function and purpose of the pamper pole, our ropes course specialist provided one more measure of readiness. He told me how to put on a special harness, and he explained the concept and the practice of *belaying*, essential to all ropes course high elements. The harness I wore fit around my legs and waist, and a very strong rope ran through an equally strong loop in the harness near my navel, through something called a carabiner (a metal fixture that prevented the rope from snarling), up through another carabiner attached to a super sturdy cable that ran from one tree near the pamper pole to another tree a short distance from the pamper pole, and back down to the specialist, who wore a harness just like mine with a carabiner just like mine, through which ran the very same rope.

We were connected. And we were connected in such way that were I to falter while making my climb, while contemplating my gravity-defying leap, or while hoping in midair that my nervousness would not exceed my ability to reach and grasp the trapeze, I would be safe because I was *on belay*.

While willingly and readily engaged in the pamper pole challenge, the ropes course specialist would be vigilantly monitoring my every move and diligently attending to the rope that connected him to me and us to the wire above. And in the event that I lost my footing, a handhold, or fell short of the trapeze, the specialist was in position to use his weight and the leverage of the belay system to safely suspend me in midair and gently lower me back to terra firma. The specialist added that even more security can be added to the belay system by having others (usually those waiting their turn) hold a section of the belay rope, one after the other in a line extending from the climber. The combined vigilance and leverage of a whole group dedicated to the safety of the climber foster a strong sense of security and trust.

With a clear sense of security added to my willingness and readiness to scale the pamper pole, off I went, harness fastened, helmet on, into the sky. After reaching the top, and fumbling my way atop the tiny platform of the now swaying pole, I achieved what felt like minimally sufficient balance to try for the trapeze. I then moved into a semi-squatting position and prepared to leap. Friends who had gathered for the inaugural event cheered me on. And on I went, pushing down hard with both feet against the platform to create the thrust I would need to reach the trapeze.

And in the same instant that I launched from the platform, the platform gave way, breaking apart under my feet. Instead of shooting out towards the trapeze, I went where gravity determined I should go, straight down, instantly, shockingly. I remember hearing gasps and hoping I was too high up and well-helmeted for my friends to see the terror on my face. It was a startling and scary moment. I was falling to the ground from a height that promised severe injury at best.

And then I wasn't. In glorious heroic defiance of the law of gravity, the ropes course specialist had gripped the rope, ending my plummet and suspending me in midair by using the belay rope. I experienced a tug and a stop, and I heard more gasps as I executed an involuntary pinwheel and then instinctively grabbed the rope to right myself.

Once lowered to the ground, I thanked the ropes course specialist effusively for, well, saving my life, and he, equally effusively, apologized for not realizing that the pamper pole platform was not as sturdy as it needed to be.

"That's OK," I said. "That's why you wanted to test it. It made the whole adventure even more fun. I knew you had me."

Three essential elements of constructive social issues discourse can be distilled from this tale of establishing sufficient safety to take virtuous risks.

1. A *willingness* on the part of the participant to engage in what can be a less-than-comfortable experience.

    Individuals declare willingness to take part in social issues discourse by knowing what it is they have signed up for. Knowing what it is they signed up for requires clear and concrete information about the discourse (college course, conference, training, etc.) provided by the purveyor (teacher, facilitator, speaker, etc.).

    The provision of clear and concrete information about the given social issues discourse (e.g. a course description) should make it possible for prospective participants to know if they are or are not willing to take part. For example, a course in water rescue techniques that will take place outside in the middle of winter is a course that some hearty souls might and some less hearty souls might not be willing to sign up for.

2. A *readiness* to participate founded on clear and sufficient preparatory explanation of the functions and purposes of the experience and a self-assessment by the potential participant of the relevant qualities he, she, or they bring to the discourse.

    Information that suffices to empower individuals to determine willingness, however, is not necessarily sufficient for them to feel *ready* to participate. Readiness in this sense requires adequate *preparation*. Four key means of preparing participants for social issues discourse are recommended. First, individuals should be given a clear forecast of the kinds of things they will likely experience in the discourse. Second, they should be guided to self-assess and monitor aspects of themselves they bring to the discourse that are likely to have a bearing on their experience and the group experience. Third, a clear set of expectations for comportment must be determined, discussed, understood, and agreed upon. Fourth, a fundamental common understanding and ability to apply basic critical thinking to social issues and the discussion of them must be established.

3. A means and methodology by which *basic safety* (belay) is provided by the facilitator/instructor/supervisor.

    Too often, deliberately remaining neutral to the dynamics between participants characterizes facilitation of social issues experiences. Such a stance usually stems from a belief that some friction between participants and allowing space for them to work things through directly and more or less on their own is useful. But this misguided principle frequently results in emotionally charged expressions on the part of some participants and reflexive protective withdrawal on the part of others and that can create a toxic mix of misunderstanding, frustration, vulnerability, and anger that results in real injury. Consistent with the pamper pole metaphor, facilitators of experiences that involve exploration of complicated and controversial social issues must be prepared to fulfil their responsibility to shift from observing and allowing space to intervening decisively to keep everyone safe.

The term "safe space," has become a lightning rod. It's an idea that motivates some to vigorously advocate that it be taken seriously and uncompromisingly integrated into situations involving the presentation of material or exchanges of views that might be upsetting to anyone. It has also led some to react with derision and contempt for people seen as unable to accept or cope with views that fall outside of their comfort zone. This polarization is unfortunate and unnecessary. After all, would anyone really advocate that interpersonal engagement on social issues (or about anything, for that matter) should be *unsafe*?

Lost in the fractious debate about safe space is the crucial concept of virtuous risk-taking. Engagement in explorations or discussions of social issues ought not be death-defying propositions, but neither should they be expected to be 100 percent comfortable, predictable, or satisfying. There is no virtue in setting oneself up for harm, and growth or enlightenment are unlikely to occur if one remains forever insulated in an echo chamber of familiar mindsets and biases. The middle ground – the common ground – of *safe enough space* is established when an individual is given sufficient information to make a meaningful choice about whether or not to participate in interactions involving social issues. Willing participants deserve to be readied for the experience they've consented to take part in. And those in roles that include oversight, supervision, authority, facilitation, teaching, coaching, or otherwise guiding the social issues process are obliged to intervene when necessary to preserve the safety of any individual in need and of the group as a whole.

Touchstone/Tool #3: The Social Identity Prism

As introduced and explained in Chapter 2, the Social Identity Prism is a unified and unifying framework of understanding and approaching all matters involving social identity, social bias, and social justice, and diversity, equity, and inclusivity. The Social Identity Prism is discussed here as an effective tool to enable users to understand and activate the following:

1. *A wholistic, intersectional, and coalitional approach to understanding and addressing social bias:*

Example: Consider examples of how solidarity, advocacy, and resistance to social bias tend to operate for each Prism social identity category (e.g., rallies, slogans, legislation – gay pride, black lives matter, women's rights, etc.). Imagine how resistance to social bias might be different if no matter which social identity category were the focus of bias, all aspects of social identity were always brought to bear on a given situation so that whole, irreducible personhood was always kept in sight, and the goal of ending social bias in all its forms was the unifying, inclusive banner under which everyone mobilized.

2. *Personal reflection:*

Example: Create a personal identity map using the Prism. List your own identity categories such as racialization, gender, sexuality, ability, and religion. For each category, consider whether or not your personal identity matches your social identity. Write down how you think each social identity category has shaped your experiences, privileges, and challenges. This self-reflective exercise can illuminate how different aspects of your identity impact your life and your interactions with others.

3. *Understanding others:*

Example: In a team setting, if there is confidence that it can be done without putting anyone in an awkward, isolative position (and/or setting them up to represent everyone who shares the given social identity), invite members to share stories about a significant experience related to one aspect of their social identity. Use the Prism to discuss how their identity might have influenced the outcome of their story. This promotes empathy and a deeper understanding of the diversity within the group. If it's best not to use personal stories of group members, consider the stories of well-known historical or other figures (e.g., athletes, artists, leaders, etc.).

4. *Identifying biases:*

Example: Conduct a workshop where participants are presented with various scenarios involving decision-making with people from diverse backgrounds (e.g., hiring, renting an apartment, or buying a house). These scenarios could range from hiring decisions, customer service interactions, to everyday personal choices. For example, one scenario might involve choosing a leader for a project based on brief bios that subtly hint at the candidates' social identities.

After each scenario, ask them to identify where bias (social advantages and social disadvantages) may have played a role and how the Social Identity Prism could help reveal underlying prejudices.

5. *Facilitating DEI conversations:*

Example: During DEI training, discussion of student behavior or performance, or consideration of how a parent is responding to a teacher or topic, use the Prism as a framework to prevent reductive or biased interpretations and treatment. Ask participants to consider how the student's social identity could affect their behavior and performance. For example, could cultural background influence their participation in class discussions? Discuss how a parent's social identity and experiences might shape their response to a teacher or school policy. Are there potential cultural or socioeconomic factors influencing their perspective? This can help participants understand the layered complexities of identity and how they can affect individuals and organizational culture.

6. *Educational framework:*

Example: Teachers can use the Prism as a basis for lesson plans that explore historical figures, cultures, and events. By examining these topics through the Prism, students can consider the multifaceted nature of social identities and their relevance in history and society.

7. *DEI-expansive policy development:*

Example: When creating or updating organizational policies, use the Prism to ensure that different social identities are considered. For example, when drafting a non-discrimination policy, the Prism can be a guide to ensure that all relevant aspects of identity are explicitly protected.

8. *Inclusive decision-making:*

Example: When considering the make-up, scope, and purview of work, and meeting expectations of a board or parent-teacher association, use the Prism to remain vigilant to everything from creating a diverse membership, to being sensitive to differences in capacities to contribute time and money, to when and where meetings should be held to achieve equitable access and participation.

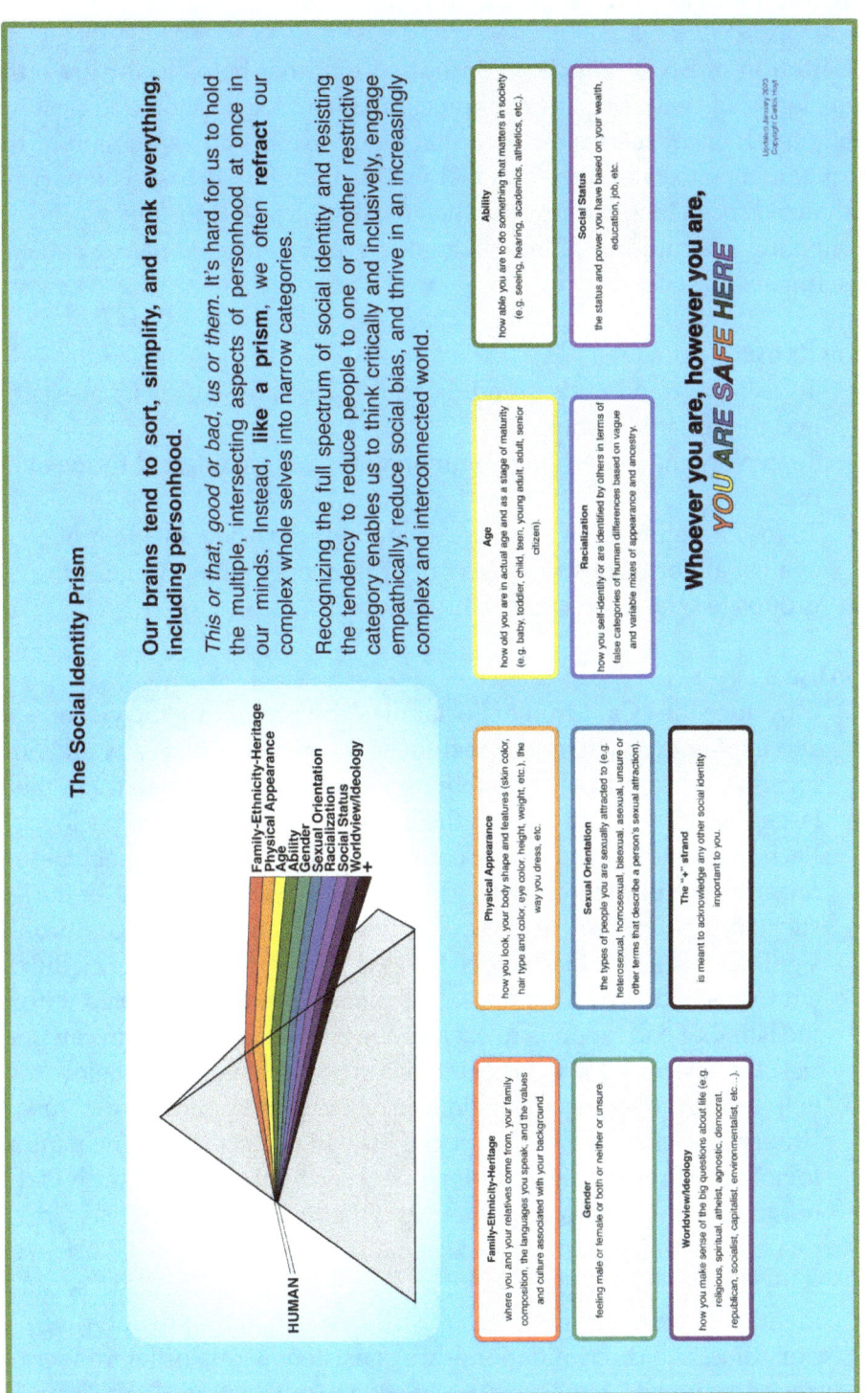

Figure 2.1 The Social Identity Prism

Touchstone/Tool #4: The Cauldron of Social Bias

The Cauldron of Social Bias is a conceptual tool that helps to illustrate the various forms of social bias, from ethnocentrism and xenophobia to classism and bigotry. It encapsulates the idea that every 'ism' is an expression of the human tendency to categorize and hierarchize individuals based on narrow, essentialized social identity groups. The visual depicts various forms of social bias bubbling in a cauldron, symbolizing their interconnected nature and collective impact on society.

Goals of Its Use
- To recognize and understand the pervasive nature of social biases and their manifestations.
- To explore the underlying commonalities across different forms of bias.
- To foster a mindset of allyship, encouraging participants to unite against all forms of social bias rather than only advocating for the groups to which they personally belong.

How to Use It
1. Introduce the "Cauldron of Social Bias" by presenting the visual and explaining each term it includes. The visual depicts any and all forms of social bias as the bubbling, oozing purple substance in the large cauldron floating above the array of smaller cauldron below. Each smaller cauldron on the conveyor belt represents social bias focused on a particular social identity group. The sameness of the substance poured into each small cauldron from the large cauldron signifies that social bias is social bias is social bias. It just takes different forms in different contexts. Each small cauldron is labeled with the ism that corresponds to each of the Social Identity Prism categories. Use the Social Bias is Social Bias is Social Bias section below to help learners/participants gain a strong understanding of the transitivity of social bias. That is, social bias, in essence, is the inclination to hold prejudiced/bigoted views or discriminate against individuals based on perceived differences, whether those differences are related to ethnicity, appearance, racialization gender, sexual orientation, ability, age, religion, social status, or any other aspect of social identity. The underlying mechanisms of social bias – stereotyping, prejudice, and discrimination – are consistent across different identities and contexts. However, the specific manifestations, targets, and impacts of such biases can vary significantly.

2. Facilitate a discussion about how these biases are not isolated issues but are interrelated varieties of social bias, a broader fundamental societal challenge.
3. Encourage participants to share observations about the form-and-substance nature of social bias (forms vary, but social bias is social bias).
4. Discuss the concept of allyship as defined by the tool (coalitional, not competitive), drawing parallels to the NATO definition where individuals treat threats to allies as threats to themselves, ready to defend others as they would themselves ("The Alliance is founded on the principle of collective defence, meaning that if one NATO Ally is attacked, then all NATO Allies are attacked."[1]). Use the "Ally" or "Co-conspirator"? section below to help learners/participants determine their bearing of which term best describes an active coalitional and collaborative approach to preventing and addressing social bias.

Social Bias Is Social Bias Is Social Bias

In our journey towards understanding and dismantling the mechanisms that perpetuate division and inequality, it's crucial to grasp a fundamental truth: social bias is social bias is social bias. This statement underscores the notion that any form of discrimination, regardless of the social identity group it targets, threatens the very fabric of peaceful coexistence. It's a call to recognize and challenge the insidious nature of social bias that infiltrates our interactions, institutions, and internal belief systems.

Social bias stems from the erroneous belief in a hierarchy of social identities, where certain attributes, whether visible or invisible, are falsely conflated with essential differences that could, in some twisted logic, justify unequal treatment. This misapprehension leads to discrimination, marginalization, and a perpetuation of injustice against various social identity groups. Whether these groups are defined by race, gender, sexuality, ability, or any other characteristic, the underlying dynamic of perceived superiority and inferiority remains the same.

The origins of this dynamic are as varied as they are historical, rooted in chance and circumstance rather than any factual basis for superiority or inferiority. Over time, countless social identity groups have found themselves alternately vilified or valorized, based on shifting societal norms, power structures, and the paranoia or whims of those in control. This arbitrariness is a clear indicator that no inherent justification exists for such bias; it is a product of social construction rather than natural differentiation.

Embracing and employing critical thinking is essential in combating social bias. It allows us to see beyond the superficial differences that divide us, recognizing our shared humanity and the inherent dignity of every individual.

Critical thinking challenges us to question the every-social-identity-group-for-itself status quo, to look critically at the narratives we've been taught, and to dismantle the structures that uphold inequality. It's about understanding that social bias, in any form, is a distortion of reality, a barrier to justice, and a threat to our collective well-being.

The recognition of social bias as a universal threat enables and compels us to take action to prevent, resist, combat, and ultimately end social bias in all its manifestations.

Imagine All the People Standing Up for Equality

Understanding that "social bias is social bias is social bias" is more than a mantra; it's a recognition of our shared responsibility to forge a world where every individual can exist free from the shadows of prejudice and discrimination. It's an acknowledgment that our destinies are intertwined, that the liberation of one is tied to the liberation of all. By committing to this understanding and taking action against social bias, we pave the way for a future marked by justice, equity, and genuine peace.

"Ally" or "Co-conspirator"?

As you reflect on the Cauldron of Social Bias, let's delve into what it means to stand against bias. You may have heard the terms "ally" and "co-conspirator" used in social justice conversations.

An ally is someone who supports and stands up for others, but some argue this can imply an otherwise passive role or a position of privilege. The term "co-conspirator" suggests active engagement, yet it carries a connotation of secrecy, scheming, or wrongdoing, which may not be conducive to the aboveboard transparency we would wish for in social justice efforts.

The concept of allyship within NATO (National Allied Treaty Organization) is built around collective defense and mutual support, with each member pledging to consider an armed attack against one member as an attack against all. This idea of shared responsibility and defense parallels the concept of social allyship where one stands up against bias or injustice directed at another as if it were directed at oneself. The analogy, though not exact, emphasizes a commitment to proactive support and defense in solidarity with others. This form of allyship goes beyond passive support to active and engaged defense of others' rights and dignity, similar to NATO's collective defense principle.

The understanding of allyship as used in the Cauldron of Social Bias visual and as promoted in our conceptualization of an antibias approach aligns with a collaborative, equitable form of support that transcends a hierarchical savior complex. It emphasizes mutual aid and reciprocal support, which is an active, constructive approach to allyship. It suggests a partnership where support is given as part of a community, rather than from a position of power over those being supported. This perspective on allyship stresses active participation and shared struggle against injustice, which is essential for effective social change.

Consider these perspectives, and then think about how you see your role in confronting bias. Do you feel more aligned with the active supportive presence of an ally or the furtive, conniving stance of a co-conspirator? Or perhaps there's a different term or concept that better captures your approach to acting against bias.

Your goal is to define for yourself the most authentic and effective way to contribute to a world free from social bias. This is not just about choosing a term but about understanding and committing to the actions and attitudes that embody that role.

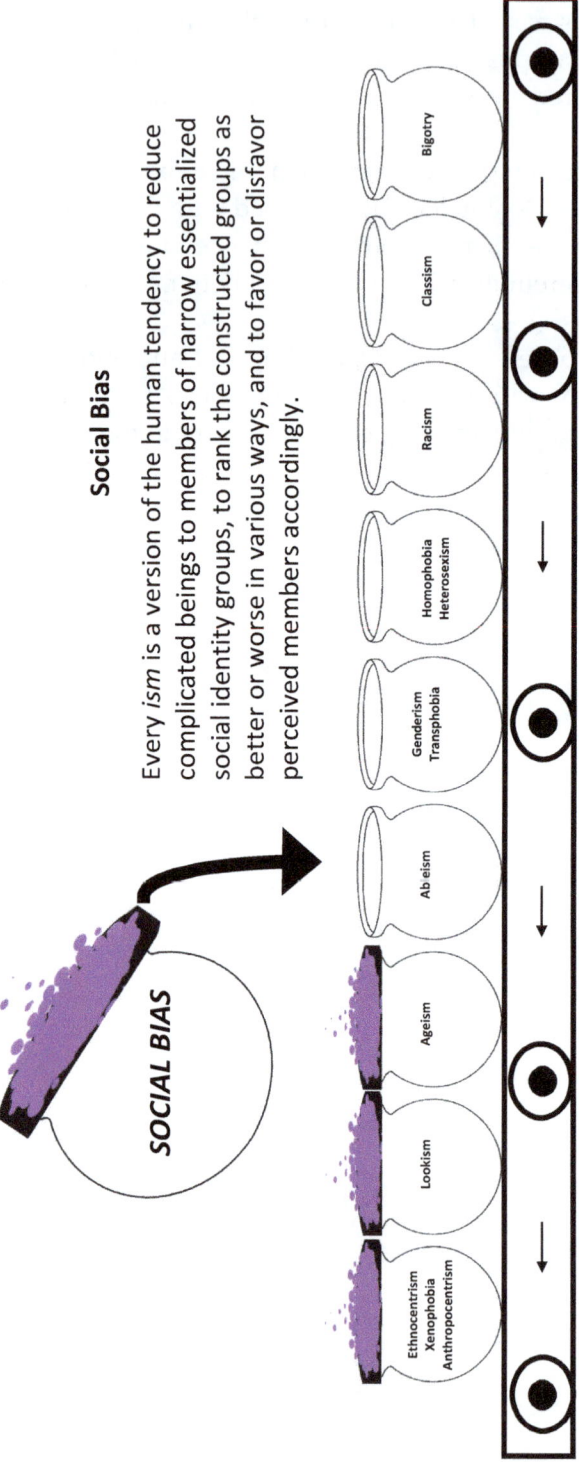

Figure 2.2 The Cauldron of Social Bias

Touchstone/Tool #5: The DEI Ally Pact (Adult and Young Student Versions)

A DEI Ally Pact is a commitment or agreement (a 'pact') that an individual makes to act as an ally in the context of Diversity, Equity, and Inclusivity (DEI). It's a personal statement that acknowledges one's own limitations and biases while affirming a commitment to overcoming them and acting in support of others.

The first version – the one that features *blocked, tough*, and *blank* spots – will likely be suitable for adults, high school students, and possibly middle-schoolers. The other version is recommended for students who will benefit from less metaphorical and more direct language.

DEI Ally Pact Learning and Activation Plan
Objective: To understand and commit to the DEI Ally Pact through self-reflection, dialogue, and mutual agreements.

I. Introduction (10 Minutes)
1. Clarifying the DEI Ally Pact, its objectives, and its significance.
2. Whole group discussion of the key terms: *blocked spots, tough spots, blank spots, work to do*, and their implications in our interactions with others.

II. Small Group Discussion (30 Minutes)

A. Personal Reflection (5 Minutes)
Each participant silently considers the DEI Ally Pact and reflects on the following:
1. Which aspects (*blocked, tough, blank* spots, *work to do*) resonate most with you, and why?
2. Recall a moment when you might have displayed one of these aspects.
3. Recall a moment when you interacted with someone who was stuck in a blocked, tough, or blank spot or was neglecting to do work they should do.
4. How your own social identities (referencing the Social Identity Prism categories) might influence the Ally Pact dimensions.
5. How you perceive the Ally pact aspects might factor into interactions with colleagues, students, and parents of different backgrounds.

B. Triads Discussion (15 Minutes)
Each person shares their responses to the Personal Reflection prompts.

C. Whole Group Discussion (10–15 Minutes)
Share Insights
1. Representatives from each triad share their group's insights and reflections.
2. Open floor for additional thoughts, feelings, and reactions to shared insights.

III. Role-Playing Activity (20 Minutes)
Volunteers role-play scenarios where they exhibit blocked, tough, or blank spots in interactions. Choose a situation from item A3 to role-play for about five minutes. Have one person enact the blocked, tough, blank, or work to do aspects, and then have the other group members respond with what they would say to constructively respond.

After the role-play, discuss the following:
1. What aspects of the responses were most effective, and why?
2. What could have been done differently to respond most effectively?
3. How did social identities come into play in these situations?

IV. Personal Commitment (5–8 Minutes)

A. Writing Exercise
Participants spend a few minutes writing down the following:
1. One personal Pact-related commitment they'll make based on today's discussion (e.g., discuss it with parents, students, or colleagues and encourage them to approach you with observations if they feel your behavior represents and aspect of the Pact)
2. How they will hold themselves accountable to the DEI Ally Pact in their interactions

B. Optional Sharing (8–10 Minutes)
Willing and ready participants share their commitments with the group.

V. Considering the Student Version of the DEI Ally Pact

A. Assessing Developmental Fit
1. Which version of the Pact would be most suitable for the students you work with?
2. How might you involve students in making this determination?

B. Developing a Lesson Plan to Introduce the Pact to Students
1. How might you adapt this approach to learning about and discussing the DEI Ally Pact to make it suitable for your students?

C. Whole Group Discussion (8–10 Minutes)
Share ideas and questions about engaging students in considering the DEI Ally Pact.

VI. Closing (10 Minutes)

A. Group Reflection Discussion
How can we support each other in upholding our commitments to the DEI Ally Pact?

B. Recap and Call to Action
1. Recognize and embrace the ongoing nature of this work.
2. Exemplify open communication, humility, and a commitment to learning.
3. Create and post visible reminders to activate the benefits of the DEI Ally Pact.
4. Create a method of continuous monitoring of actions associated with the DEI Ally Pact – ways to know that community members are putting the Pact to work to create and maintain a truly inclusive environment.

DEI Ally Pact Student Version Key Terms
Pact: a pact is a strong agreement between people.

Ally: an ally is someone who is ready and willing to see someone else's challenges as if they were their own and partner with them to overcome the challenges.

Diversity: diversity means variety – different kinds of objects, people, ideas, etc. A group of people can be diverse in many ways. When we are thinking in terms of diversity, equity, and inclusivity, diversity refers to a group of people with different social identities and the different perspectives, customs, and talents that might be associated with them.

Equity: equity describes efforts to provide individuals or groups with what they need in order to have opportunities and basic needs met on par with those of other individuals or groups. Equality is about things being the same. For example, giving everyone going on a bike ride a bicycle represents equality. Giving each person a bicycle that fits them represents equity. Making sure a building has safe stairs from floor to floor for everyone is equality. Making sure there are ramps and elevators for people who need them to get from floor to floor is equity.

Inclusivity: inclusivity is about making sure that every member of a community feels as safe, respected, and valued as other members in the community. Every community cannot be expected to include every possible person (there are often reasonable qualifications to become a member of a community), but everyone who qualifies and is accepted into a community has the right to feel a healthy sense of belonging.

Social Identity: social identity is how we think of ourselves in terms of being a member of social identity groups (e.g., family-ethnicity-heritage, physical appearance, age, ability, gender, sexual orientation, racialization, status, and worldview/ideology).

Accidentally: accidents are unexpected, unintended, and often unfortunate incidents.

Defensive: to be defensive is to act as if one is under attack, which can lead to retreating, freezing up, or counterattacking.

Student DEI Ally Pact Key Terms

Diversity: diversity means variety – different kinds of objects, people, ideas, etc. A group of people can be diverse in many ways. When we are thinking in terms of diversity, equity, and inclusivity, diversity refers to a group of people with different social identities and the ways people are treated based on how others define and judge their social identities.

Equity: equity describes efforts to provide individuals or groups with what they need in order to have opportunities, resources, safety, health, etc. equal to those of other individuals or groups.

Equality is about things being the same. For example, giving everyone going on a bike ride a bicycle represents equality. Giving each person a bicycle that fits them represents equity. Making sure a building has safe stairs from floor to floor for everyone is equality. Making sure there are ramps and elevators for people who need them to get from floor to floor is equity.

Inclusivity: inclusivity is about making sure that every member of a community feels as safe, respected, and valued as other members in the community. Every community cannot be expected to include every possible person (there are often reasonable qualifications to become a member of a community) but everyone who qualifies and is accepted into a community has the right to feel a healthy sense of belonging.

Social Identity: social identity is how we think of ourselves in terms of being a member of social identity groups (e.g., family-ethnicity-heritage, physical appearance, age, ability, gender, sexual orientation, racialization, status, and worldview/ideology).

Ally: an ally is someone who is ready and willing to see someone else's challenges as if they were their own and partner with them to overcome the challenges.

Pact: a pact is a strong agreement between people.

Accidentally: accidents are unexpected, unintended, and often unfortunate incidents.

Defensive: to be defensive is to act as if one is being threatened or attacked – to protect oneself from something the feels harmful.

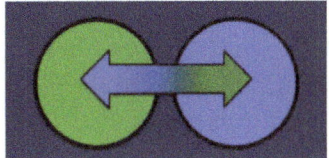

My Diversity Equity & Inclusivity Ally Pact

I know I have **blocked** spots
- the inability to see that what I'm doing might be harmful to someone -

I know I have **tough** spots
- the natural resistance to input that suggests
my behavior conflicts with my intention-

I know I have **blank** spots
- a lack of data and knowledge about crucial differences
in social advantages and disadvantages between myself and others -

I know *I have work to do*
I promise to do the work I need to do to see my biases, spare you my defensiveness, and educate myself in order to be the most effective teacher/student/parent/family member/employer/employee/colleague/partner/friend/citizen I can be.

I hope you will always feel entitled to let me know if my blind, tough, or blank spots ever cause you to feel anything less than respected, included, and well-served by me. I promise to always do my best to receive your notice of my mistakes with humility and gratitude.

Figure 2.3 The DEI Ally Pact – Adults

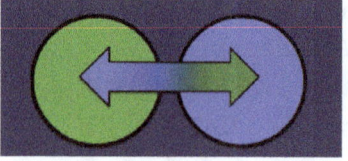

My Diversity Equity & Inclusivity Ally Pact

I know I might hurt your feelings *accidentally*
Something I do might feel fine to me but it might not feel good to you

I know I might get *defensive*
It can be hard for anyone to learn that they did something they didn't mean to do

I know *I don't know* everything about everyone
Being in diverse communities means there's always more to learn about the people we're with

I know *I have work to do*
It's my responsibility to avoid accidentally hurting you, not to be defensive, and to learn as much as I can about the people in my communities so that I can be the best friend, classmate, teammate, and partner I can be

I *promise*
I hope you will always feel entitled to let me know if I hurt you or get defensive or need to learn something to help you feel safe, seen, and respected. I promise to always do my best to be humble and grateful if you give me the gift of your honesty.

Figure 2.4 The DEI Ally Pact – Students

Touchstone/Tool # 6: Input, Influence, and Individual Choice: Exploring the Relationship Between Socialization and Personal Choice

Social identity constructs are immediately ascribed and continuously reinforced. Ultimately, your sense of self is determined by the manner in which you synthesize how society identifies you (ascription) and how you identify yourself (subscription). From birth, we receive input about how to think about identity from many sources. Some inputs are powerfully influential and become constructions of identity that guide our beliefs and actions. Others might not *stick*. The extent to which and manner in which we identify with these constructs determines the definition of our multidimensional self. We are not completely malleable and passive as society exerts its shaping forces. Every individual brings temperaments, proclivities, and choices to the dynamic interaction with external forces. *Genes + Environment + Chance + Choice = YOU.*

In "Becoming: Basic Considerations for a Psychology of Personality," pioneering psychologist Gordon Allport pointed out the following truth about cultural/social conditioning and personal choice.

> That the cultural approach yields valuable facts we cannot possibly deny, for culture is indeed a major condition in becoming. <u>Yet personal integration is always the more basic fact</u>. While we accept certain cultural values as propriate, as important for our own course of becoming, it is equally true that we are all rebels, deviants, and individualists. Some elements in our culture we reject altogether; many we adopt as mere opportunistic habits, and even those elements we genuinely appropriate we refashion to fit our own personal style of life. Culture is a condition of becoming but it is not the full stencil.[2]

We're born into the world ready to learn, and we're born into a world ready to teach us plenty. Even before we emerge, society has designs on us. Perhaps the most powerful input we get from our socializing sources has to do with how to think about social identity. We enter into a world that promotes placing people in social identity groups. As illustrated in the Social Identity Prism (discussed in Chapter 3), those groups include family-ethnicity-heritage, physical appearance, age, ability, gender, sexual orientation, racialization, social status, and worldview/ideology.

Social identity group categories define/construct our similarities with and differences from others and serve as the basis for stereotypes and prejudice, intra-group connection, inter-group conflict, unearned privilege, and unfair discrimination (as illustrated in the Cauldron of Social Bias in Chapter 3). This is why it's crucial that we understand where our bearing on social identities (our own social identities and those of others come from). By examining the multiple sources that provide input into our beliefs and behaviors about social identities, identifying which sources have been most influential, and recognizing our inevitable opportunity and responsibility to determine our own bearing, we will do the best we can to interact constructively with others.

The Input, Influence, and Individual Choice exercise will give you an opportunity to see how your bearing on social identity groups has been shaped by powerful socializing forces throughout your life, and, most importantly, how you have chosen to adopt, adapt, or reject constructs, beliefs, and behaviors you've been exposed to.

The Inputs, Influences, and Individual Choices Worksheet provides space for you to note what you consider to be the primary messages you were given about each of the Social Identity Prism social identity categories. Some of the messages might have been conveyed clearly and explicitly, and some may have been communicated more implicitly, perhaps through role models in your life. In each case, please try to note the primary messages you received from mezzo sources and from macro sources, after which you can express your micro synthesis of the mezzo and macro inputs.

Mezzo refers to the many groups or communities in your life, from the moment you were born (e.g., family and care providers) to your school years (e.g., teachers, peers, school materials), to sources such as religious, spiritual, or secular moral communities (e.g., faith communities, or secular humanist organizations), to sports teams or recreational groups, to regional influences, and so on. *Macro* refers to larger sources and forces that have society-wide reach, such as the media, the government, and pop culture. *Micro* refers to your personal, individual synthesis of your mezzo and macro inputs.

It's natural to adopt the views, values, and conduct of those who raise us, particularly when we are very young and likely without points of comparison or exposure to alternative ways of understanding the world – but it's certainly not inevitable. As we mature and our circles of experience become wider and wider, it's very likely that we will encounter different cultural and social beliefs and behaviors than those that were prominent and primary during our upbringing. Such encounters create opportunities to consider new ways of thinking and behaving, and such considerations can lead to a conscious decision to preserve and perpetuate what we were taught or to modify or even reject some of what we were taught.

Inputs, Influences, and Individual Choices Worksheet, Example, and Prompts

Social Identity Category: Family-Ethnicity-Heritage
    Mezzo-level input:
    Macro-level input:
    My micro-level bearing:

Social Identity Category: Physical Appearance
    Mezzo-level input:
    Macro-level input:
    My micro-level bearing:
    Social Identity Category: Age
    Mezzo-level input:
    Macro-level input:
    My micro-level bearing:

Social Identity Category: Ability
    Mezzo-level input:
    Macro-level input:
    My micro-level bearing:

Social Identity Category: Gender
    Mezzo-level input:
    Macro-level input:
    My micro-level bearing:

Social Identity Category: Sexual Orientation
    Mezzo-level input:
    Macro-level input:
    My micro-level bearing:

Social Identity Category: Racialization
    Mezzo-level input:
    Macro-level input:
    My micro-level bearing:

Social Identity Category: Social Status
    Mezzo-level input:
    Macro-level input:
    My micro-level bearing:

Social Identity Category: Worldview/Ideology
   Mezzo-level input:
   Macro-level input:
   My micro-level bearing:

Social Identity Category: The "+" Category – representing another social identity category that matters to you and that doesn't seem to be represented in the Social Identity Prism
   Mezzo-level input:
   Macro-level input:
   My micro-level bearing:

Example: Social Identity Category: Family-Ethnicity-Heritage
Mezzo-level input: From a very early age, I'm sure before I could even understand or remember, my family taught us to be super proud of where we're from, our traditions, food . . . everything associated with being our ethnicity. I realized after a while that many families do this regarding their heritage too. Sadly, in my family, and in so many I know, feeling great about your identity is too often paired with thinking poorly of other people's background. I can remember almost as many put-downs of other social identity groups as positive comments about ours.

Macro-level input: I feel that the United States gives a lot of messages about ethnicity. We should be proud of our ethnicity – and we might even have a day or week or month dedicated to it. We should be proud of being an "immigrant nation," and we should be proud of being American as its own kind of ethnicity. At the same time, we aren't always welcoming of people from different places, and there's a lot of friction sometimes between different ethnicities and cultures.

My micro-level bearing: As I've gotten older, it feels impossible to not have a sense of almost reflex pride in my heritage, but I also try hard to resist thinking or acting as if my background is any better than anyone else's. I also learned that pretty much everyone has DNA bits and pieces from many regions of the planet in them, and that ultimately, we all are from Africa as well as all the places our ancestors spent some time in. For me that's a cool thing. Something that I hope can maybe break down some false barriers between us that lead to needless conflicts.

Touchstone/Tool #7: Empathy: The other "E" in DEI

Empathy should be considered the other "E" in DEI. DEI-expansivism requires empathy – the capacity to accurately comprehend the feelings of others. Empathy is the bridge that allows us to traverse the gap between our own lived experiences and preferences and those of individuals whose life stories, backgrounds, and preferences may significantly diverge from our own. Empathy is a *feelings X-ray* that equips us to base our assessment of and reaction to people's views and behavior on an accurate understanding – a proper *seeing* – of the feelings that underpin belief and behavior.

In the dynamic interplay of social identity, social bias, and social justice, empathy emerges not as a passive emotional response, but as an active tool for understanding. It enables us to decenter from our own subjective viewpoints and perceive the world through someone else's lens – not necessarily to *sympathize* with them (to feel in agreement with and share their feelings), and not necessarily to endorse the behavior that stems from their feelings, but simply and powerfully to understand the feelings and thereby avoid basing our responses on misunderstandings.

Empathy is prerequisite to cultural proficiency, competency, social justice, and plain old getting along with others. If we're not teaching our children how to understand and make use of empathy, we're neglecting to provide essential foundational preparation for respectful, civil, peaceful interaction.

Understanding Empathy

> The state of empathy, or being empathic, is to perceive the internal frame of reference of another with accuracy and with the emotional components and meanings which pertain thereto as if one were the person, but without ever losing the "as if" condition. Thus it means to sense the hurt or the pleasure of another as he senses it and to perceive the causes thereof as he perceives them, but without ever losing the recognition that it is as if I were hurt or pleased and so forth. If this "as if" quality is lost, then the state is one of identification.
>
> Rogers, 1995, p. 140[3]

A psychotherapy practice student of Carlos's once uttered this eureka moment realization about empathy:

> Now I get it! Empathy is like being inside someone else's ocean but with your wet suit on! You're inside their feelings, but *their* feelings

aren't *your* feelings. You have your own ocean of feelings, and your feelings about another person's feeling might be positive, negative, or neutral.

This clarity of understanding is fortified by examining the different prefixes of empathy and sympathy. The *em-* prefix of *em*pathy tends to mean *in, into/inside*. They *sym-* prefix of *sym*pathy tends to mean *with, together*. You can be inside someone's feelings, exploring them and understanding them, but that does not mean that you are also with the person in that your feelings and their feelings are interchangeable and aligned.

Empathy doesn't require that you agree with what you understand about another person. That would be *sympathy*.

Empathy doesn't require that you feel bad for someone (often someone whose lot is worse than or inferior to your own). That would be *pity*.

Empathy doesn't require that you feel sorrow for someone and a desire to come to their aid. That would be *compassion*.

Empathy doesn't even require that you do something nice for someone. That would be *kindness*.

Empathy is understanding how someone feels and how their feelings inform their actions. Period.

Empathy Works Like an X-ray

After a doctor looks at an X-ray, they know what's going on inside someone's body, and then the doctor can decide what is the best thing to do. The doctor will probably say things like "I see what's going on. I accurately understand what's going on with this part of your body." Then the doctor might decide to do nothing more and allow the person to heal on their own or the doctor might decide that they should do something to help.

Empathy is like a feelings X-ray. It shows you what's happening inside the feelings of another person. Once you're pretty sure you "see" what's going on inside another person, you can say something like, "I think understand what you're feeling." If the person ratifies your assessment, then you know you got it right.

After that, you might decide to do nothing more and allow the person to take care of themselves, or you might decide that you should do something.

But how do you find out what someone is feeling? There's no actual machine that can help us discern someone's feeling the way an X-ray can actually show what's going on inside a person's body, but empathy properly applied comes close.

Applying Empathy: The Empathic Inquiry Method – A User's Guide

As you read about the EIM, please keep in mind the following scenarios.

Scenario One

A friend, partner, colleague, or family member with whom you've enjoyed a long and mutually fulfilling relationship based on shared values and interests expresses a perspective on an issue that is nearly diametrically opposed to your perspective on the issue. To make matters more challenging, the person with whom you suddenly find yourself in conflict sees the issue as one on which there cannot be the vaunted agree to disagree resolution. Either you can come to your senses, renounce your current view and embrace theirs, or your relationship is no longer viable.

Scenario Two

One of your mentees, an adversely racialized person, and someone who is clearly qualified and competent in their area of study, is demonstrating significant trepidation when it comes to presenting their work to peers and faculty, so much so that their productivity has decreased, as has their attendance. You've ruled out competency as the possible root issue, and while anxiety seems a possible reason, you see no signs of anxiety beyond this particular issue.

The Empathic Inquiry Method (EIM) is a combination of algorithmic (four steps) and heuristic (generative wondering) efforts that facilitate understanding another person's and one's own feelings in the context of challenging interpersonal dynamics. The EIM is empathy put to work. How the EIM works is illustrated and explained in the following diagram/worksheet.

The EIM enables you to explore and analyze behavioral dynamics at the level of the feelings that underly them, allowing for actions that are informed rather than reactionary and potentially misguided.

The model employs an iceberg analogy to illustrate that what is visible on the surface (behaviors and reactions) is supported by a much larger, unseen mass of underlying factors and needs. As with the ill-fated *Titanic* which collided with an iceberg and sank on April 14, 1912, so it is when we encounter challenging interpersonal dynamics. It was not the visible portion of the iceberg that led to the *Titanic* disaster. It was the roughly 90 percent of the iceberg's mass that lay out of sight under the water's surface that made it impossible for the ship to simply push through the obstacle. Similarly, with challenging interpersonal dynamics, recognizing and understanding the mass of factors that lurk beneath the surface presentation is essential to navigating successfully around the obstacle.

132 ◆ Praxis

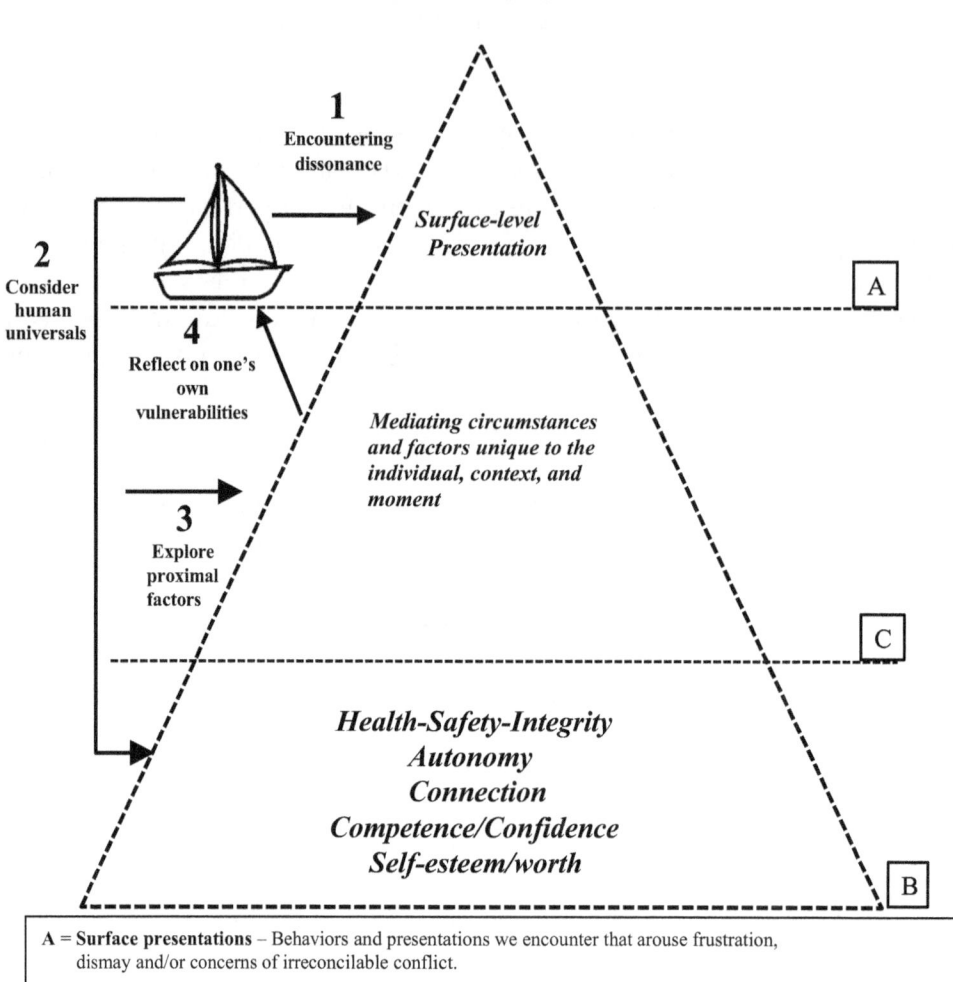

Figure 2.5 Empathic Inquiry Method Graphic #1

Here Is a Step-by-Step Breakdown of the Empathic Inquiry Method

Step 1 – Encountering Dissonance: This is the behavior that represents the visible part of the iceberg. You (represented by the sailboat that's trying to make its way to a positive destination (represented by the island oasis)) encounter a behavior or reaction in another person that may cause confusion or discomfort (labeled as "A" in the diagram).

Step 2 – Consideration of Universal Human Needs: Beneath the surface behavior are the deeper universal human needs (labeled as "B"). When these needs are threatened, they often trigger the observed surface behavior. These needs include *health, safety, integrity, autonomy, connection, competence,* and *self-worth.*

Our common susceptibility to humiliation is the only social bond that is needed.

This quote by Richard Rorty[4] delves deep into the shared human experience of vulnerability, offering a powerful reflection on empathy and social cohesion. To fully appreciate the depth of this statement, it's crucial to understand the nuanced meaning of "humiliation" beyond its common association with mere embarrassment. Humiliation, in a more profound sense, refers to the experience of having one's dignity and worth aggressively undermined or dismissed, to the point where it feels not just like a personal affront but a threat to one's very being – a mortification that touches the core of one's humanity.

This interpretation of humiliation transcends the superficial discomfort of embarrassment; it speaks to a visceral, existential fear that our inherent value as individuals is not recognized, respected, or protected. Such experiences of humiliation can evoke a profound sense of vulnerability, revealing the fragility of our social status and self-esteem. This shared vulnerability, as Rorty suggests, forms a potent social bond, for it is a condition that every person, regardless of their background or identity, can potentially experience.

Recognizing our mutual susceptibility to this deep form of humiliation fosters empathy and a sense of interconnectedness that is essential for moral and social expansivism. This approach compels us to extend our empathy and ethical considerations to include not just those within our immediate circle but also those from diverse backgrounds and experiences, fostering a more inclusive understanding of humanity.

Step 3 – Exploration of Proximal Factors: Here, you delve into the individual, contextual factors unique to the person's situation (labeled as "C"), which may be influencing their behavior at the surface level. These factors include cultural background, personal experiences, and environmental influences.

Step 4 – Self-Awareness: The final step turns the focus inward, prompting you to reflect on your own vulnerabilities and reactions to the initial behavior. This step helps to understand why you react the way you do and how your own needs and contexts might be influencing your perceptions and interactions.

134 ◆ Praxis

Using the EIM to Maximize Vigilance about Social Identity Factors

The original EIM diagram presents a general approach to navigating human behavior and responses to universal needs.

The second version incorporates the Social Identity Prism directly into the EIM, explicitly highlighting the need to consider social identity, social bias, and social justice factors that might be integral to understanding the whole picture of someone's behavior and reactions.

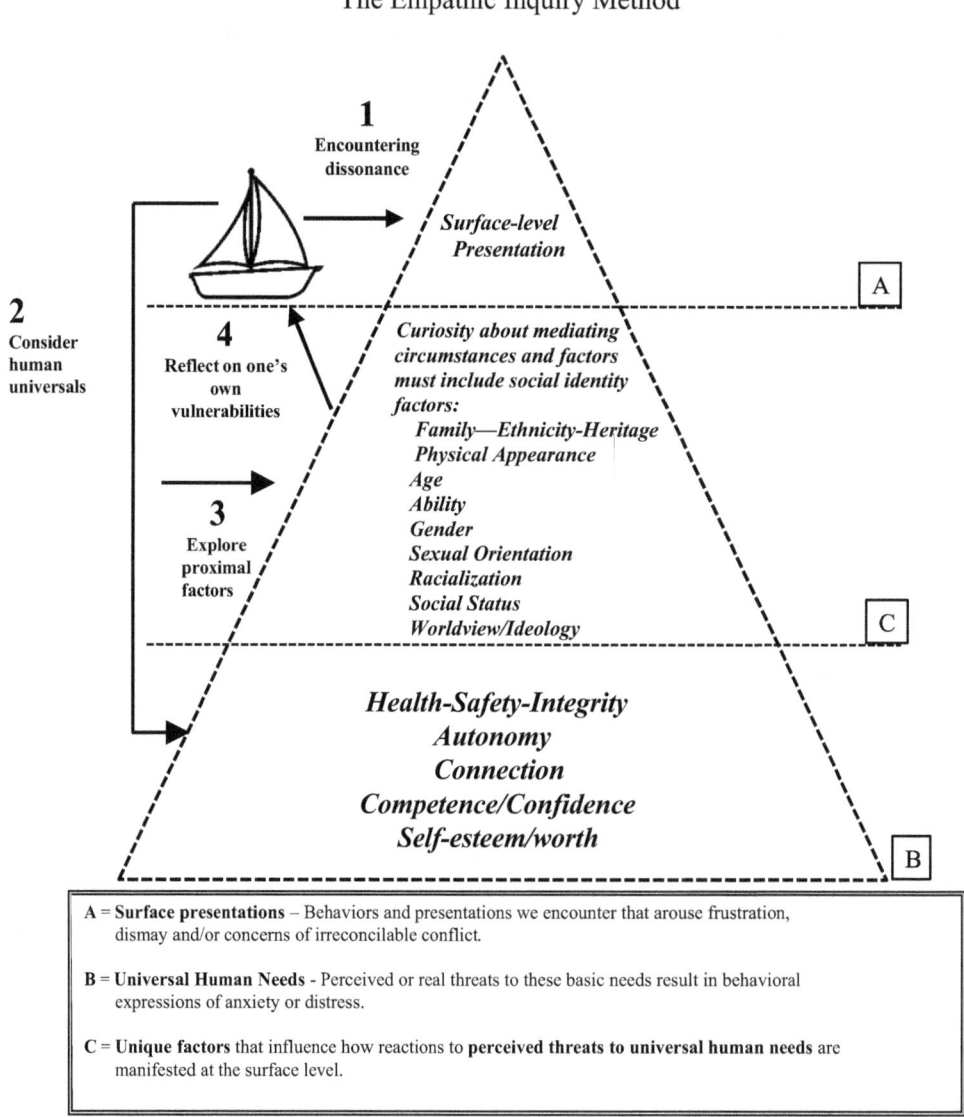

A = **Surface presentations** – Behaviors and presentations we encounter that arouse frustration, dismay and/or concerns of irreconcilable conflict.

B = **Universal Human Needs** - Perceived or real threats to these basic needs result in behavioral expressions of anxiety or distress.

C = **Unique factors** that influence how reactions to **perceived threats to universal human needs** are manifested at the surface level.

Figure 2.6 Empathic Inquiry Method Graphic #2

Using EIM with vigilance to DEI factors involves recognizing the integration of social identity categories (as seen in the second diagram) within each step of the method. Each category of the Social Identity Prism reminds you to consider how components like family, ethnicity, heritage, physical appearance, and more can compound the complexities of interpersonal dynamics. This holistic consideration is key to empathetic and effective communication and resolution in DEI contexts.

DEI-expansivism is about recognizing and responding to the universal potential for humiliation as a basis for broader moral and empathetic engagement. It challenges us to connect with others on the level of our shared human vulnerabilities, aiming to prevent the circumstances that lead to such profound feelings of worthlessness and disrespect. This perspective is vital for DEI efforts, aiming to build communities where every individual's dignity is acknowledged and safeguarded, thus reducing the instances of humiliation and its painful social and psychological consequences.

In summary, integrating a nuanced understanding of humiliation – viewing it as an existential threat to dignity and worth – into Rorty's statement emphasizes the transformative potential of empathy. It highlights how recognizing our shared vulnerability to deep-seated humiliation can serve as a foundation for social solidarity, justice, and the DEI-expansivist pursuit of a more compassionate, equitable world. This acknowledgment acts as a catalyst for DEI initiatives, guiding us toward a society where mutual respect and understanding are paramount.

Here's How You Can Use EIM to Discern Social Identity Factors That Might Pertain in Challenging Interpersonal Dynamics

Step 1: Encountering Dissonance – When you encounter challenging behaviors or presentations, observe them as just the tip of the iceberg – the part you can see. These might be moments of conflict, misunderstanding, or tension related to DEI issues. Recognize your immediate response (which is likely to be an adverse response) without judgment as a natural first step in the empathic process. Allow yourself to acknowledge your frustration, irritation, or anger when confronted with a behavior that represents and obstacle to reaching you desired goal. Later, in Step 4, you will apply the Empathic Inquiry Method to yourself to learn why you reacted to the surface presentation as you did. In steps 2 and 3, you get to be a curious detective.

Step 2: Consider Human Universals – Consider the universal human needs potentially threatened:
- Health-Safety-Integrity: Physical well-being, core beliefs, and value systems.

- Autonomy: The need for self-governance and personal agency.
- Connection: The desire for meaningful and secure relationships.
- Competence: The need to feel capable and effective.
- Self-esteem/worth: The importance of a positive self-concept and the perception of respect from others.
- Recognize these needs as potential drivers of behavior, crucial for understanding DEI challenges.

Step 3: Explore Proximal Factors – Delve into contextual factors that may shape the expression of discomfort or distress:
- Cultural nuances
- Environmental impacts
- Individual personality traits
- Historical experiences relating to social identity and biases
- Understanding these factors can illuminate why certain DEI-related behaviors manifest

Step 4: Self-Reflection – Turn the inquiry inwards. Reflect on why the behavior triggers certain emotions in you. This introspection helps identify your own needs and responses, clearing the way for a more empathetic DEI practice. Consider which of your underlying human universal needs might be or feel as if they are under threat. Reflect on your own response to the encountered behavior. What aspects of your social identity are affected? Are there biases or vulnerabilities within yourself that are being triggered? How do your own DEI-related experiences influence your perception and engagement?

Touchstone/Tool #8: Understanding and Resisting Racialization

The Race Pedagogy Dilemma: A Guide to Teaching about Racialization

Race confronts educators across all levels of learning with the challenge of teaching the truth that race is not a valid, empirical concept for subdividing human beings while living in a societal/global context dominated by *the racial worldview* – the acceptance that race, empirically real or not, is a non-negotiable way to understand human beings and human differences. This dilemma poses a significant challenge in educational settings: the need to provide information that addresses the societal impact of race and racism while also teaching the fact race is not a legitimate basis for differentiation.

As noted by one researcher on views about race in science and academia, in both (overlapping) areas, "the message that race is a social construct seem to get lost in transmission." and the view that race is somehow natural and essential to humanity prevails. Scientists and students in fields such as biology and anthropology may know that race is just a social construct (a reification of an illusion in our minds), but they talk and act as if racial differences actually exist in ways that are not correlations between circumstance and being labeled one race or another but in ways that are caused by something essentially different about people of different so-called races.[5]

Understanding race as a social construct but acting as if it indicates inherent differences is like knowing that Earth revolves around the Sun yet navigating space based on the belief that the Sun revolves around Earth. Were we to do the latter, interstellar travel would regularly result in catastrophic failure. That we have made and continue to make the analogous error regarding understanding and navigating race has and continues to result in catastrophic failure to overcome racism.

This touchstone/tool section is deliberately longer and contains more material than the other touchstone/tool sections. In order to provide an effective introduction to the crucial but little understood phenomenon of racialization, and then to equip readers with tools they can use in their pedagogy related to race, more overall material was required. The goal of this section is to help educators make the crucial shift from centering race as a real fixed central fact of human difference and recognizing racialization as the crucial process and practice that produces and sustains the false concept of race and the scourge of racism. Educators are encouraged to adapt, enhance, and otherwise tailor the content in each part of this guide to their particular circumstances.

This touchstone/tool section contains three parts that address the race pedagogy dilemma in three different ways:

1. Introducing Racialization
2. Charting a Course Beyond Racism TEDx Talk
3. The Three Jars Lesson for Young Learners

Part One – Introducing to Racialization

Warm-up Questions
1. Did you grow up in a family and society that encouraged you to believe in Santa Claus?
2. Did you know that at one time in human history, people believed the Earth must be flat?
3. Did you know that at one time in human history, people believed the Sun and the other planets near us revolved around the Earth instead of the Earth and other planets revolving around the Sun?
4. Did you know that for a long time, people thought we could understand how intelligent someone was and what they were like by examining the shape of their head?
5. Do you recall the first time the concept of race was introduced to you? What would have happened if you were never introduced to it? Would you have become aware of it on your own, like your heartbeat – something natural, real, undeniable, or might it be possible that it never would have occurred to you?

We are amazingly imaginative creatures. We are capable of creating pretty much anything in our minds – and we are capable of believing and acting as if the things we create in our minds actually exist beyond our imagination, out in the real world. We hear stories, we tell stories, we act as if some stories are facts.

The idea of race is an idea that some humans came up with about 500 years ago. It's one of the most powerful examples of an idea that people believe is a fact and act on as if it is a fact. Let's learn and think and talk about how the idea of race came about in the human mind.

Racialization
Racialization is the imaginative process by which the idea of race was created. The process has both understandable and almost innocent aspects as well as diabolical intent and lethal impact.

Seeing people as members races is, from the perspective of cognitive psychology, understandable. We are extremely prone to put things in categories. We are extremely prone to create hierarchies. We are extremely prone to confer deep meaning onto superficial differences. We are extremely prone to essentialize assumed differences – treat them as if they are natural, inevitable, and heritable.

Preracialization
The infinite range of human variation was not artificially categorized and naturalized before the advent of racialization (nascent in the late 1500s, emergent in the 1600s, and codified in America in the 1700s).

"Family, "tribe," "clan," and distinctive affiliation by other markers (such as religion or nation) have always been employed, but they were all somewhat porous, meaning that a non-group member could gain membership through, for instance, marrying in or adopting the culture of the group (e.g., language, religion, cultural practices, or pledging allegiance).

As people from different parts of the planet started to encounter each other around 400 to 500 years ago, it is somewhat understandable that our constellation of proclivities conspired to lead some minds to deduce what has come to be known as racial difference between human beings. When the then increasingly popular idea of race as science came in handy for those who sought a rationale and justification for subjugating and oppressing humans being pressed into slave labor, race rapidly shifted from pseudo-scientific speculative theory to the promulgation of truth received from authoritative figures and eventually inscribed into law.

Whether in the form of wondering about different-looking people and assuming categorical difference that are more than skin deep, pronouncing imagined differences to be empirically and scientifically valid, or exploiting spurious race science to justify economic and political oppression, racialization is the simple but powerful process by which race is reified into the basis of one of the most divisive forces in the history of human existence.

The Five Steps of the Racialization Process
Through the process of racialization – *selecting, sorting, attributing, essentializing, and acting* – the infinite range of human variability was reduced to black and white, and the fallacious borders between them became rigid and impermeable.

> Step 1 – Select some human characteristics as meaningful signs of racial difference. For example, skin color, hair texture, craniofacial features, ancestry.
> Step 2 – Sort people into factitiously homogenized human subpopulations based on selected distinctions.
> Step 3 – Attribute traits (temperament, talents, behaviors) to people according to their racial subgroups.

Step 4 – Essentialize racial differences – conceive of them as natural, immutable, and hereditary.
Step 5 – Act as if racial differences justify unequal treatment.

Race is not something you are; race is something that happens to you. After a person is racialized, they can decide to *adopt*, embrace, and endorse the imposition of identity, *adapt* it in ways that suit them, or *reject* it as the invalid notion that it is.

Race is externally imposed rather than intrinsically derived. Racialization involves categorizing individuals into specific racial groups based on perceived physical, cultural, or historical traits, which can be both arbitrary and socially constructed.

The process of racialization can significantly impact individuals and groups, influencing social dynamics, power structures, and personal identities. Once racialized, individuals face several choices:

Adoption and Embrace: Some may choose to fully embrace the racial identity assigned to them, finding community, solidarity, and strength in this identity. This can be empowering, providing a sense of belonging and a framework for interpreting experiences and organizing for social or political causes.

Selective Adaptation: Others might adopt aspects of the racial identity that resonate with them or are advantageous, while reshaping or downplaying other aspects. This selective adaptation allows for a more nuanced personal identity that can navigate various social contexts differently.

Rejection: Some individuals may reject the racial identity imposed on them altogether, seeing it as a false or oppressive construct that does not reflect their personal identity or experiences. This rejection can be a form of resistance against the simplification and stereotyping inherent in racial categorizations.

These choices highlight the dynamic nature of identity, which can be fluid and subject to change based on personal experiences, social interactions, and political consciousness. Understanding race as something that happens to an individual, rather than a fixed essence they possess, opens up discussions about the social constructions of race and the implications these constructions have on society and individuals alike. This perspective fosters a more critical view of racial dynamics and encourages a more inclusive and nuanced understanding of human diversity.

Racialization = Otherization = Alienization. The process of racialization is basically about creating a belief that some humans are so different from other humans that they are an "other" or "alien" kind of human, naturally and essentially different from other kinds of humans.

To see how the process works, and to grasp the utter arbitrariness of race categorization, use the racialization worksheets to create "races" based on the given category in each worksheet.

Racialization: How We Create Races

Step 1: SELECT some human characteristics as meaningful signs of important differences.
Step 2: SORT people into subgroups based on the characteristics.
Step 3: ATTRIBUTE traits (e.g., temperament, capacities, talents, worth) to the different groups.
Step 4: ESSENTIALIZE the differences – conceive of them as natural, fixed, unchangeable, and hereditary.
Step 5: ACT as if these differences justify unequal treatment.

Example: Racialization Worksheet – Based on Ear Shape

Step 1: SELECT some human characteristics as meaningful signs of important differences.
Attached or Detached earlobes.
Step 2: SORT people into subgroups based on the characteristics.
People with attached earlobes will be considered their own group, and people with detached earlobes will be considered their own group.
What should we do with people whose earlobes are almost totally attached but maybe just a little detached?
Step 3: ATTRIBUTE traits (e.g., temperament, capacities, talents, worth) to the different groups.
I've noticed that people with attached earlobes seem more grounded, stable, are good listeners, and stick to the rules.
I've heard that people with detached earlobes are easily distracted, bad listeners, and reckless.
Step 4: ESSENTIALIZE the differences – conceive of them as natural, fixed, unchangeable, and hereditary.
Clearly, the deep differences between attached and detached people must be somehow genetically based. Even if people with detached earlobes were to somehow get them attached, it wouldn't change their underlying nature. If a person with attached earlobes is known to have anyone in their ancestry that had detached earlobes, then they are part of the detached earlobe group.
Step 5: ACT as if these differences justify unequal treatment.
It's only logical to treat people with attached and detached earlobes differently. After all, they clearly have valuable and superior natures and characteristics compared with people who have attached earlobes.

Racialization Worksheet – Based on Height
Step 1: Select some human characteristics as meaningful signs of important differences
Step 2: Sort people into subgroups based on the characteristics.
Step 3: Attribute traits (e.g., temperament, capacities, talents, worth) to the different groups.
Step 4: Essentialize the differences – conceive of them as natural, fixed, unchangeable, and hereditary.
Step 5: Act as if these differences justify unequal treatment.
What do you think?
So how should you feel, think, and act about race based on these examples of racialization?

Believing in race as biology, and/or acting as if it is biology, leads us to overlook the social factors that contribute to inequality. Understanding that race is socially constructed is the first step in addressing those factors and giving everyone a fair chance in life.

Does this mean that everyone should stop believing in race and act as if race isn't real and doesn't matter? What about people who gain a sense of community and pride and positive identity from seeing themselves as members of a race?

Lots of people take pride in being a member of what we call a race or an ethnicity or a culture. That is why some folks express, for example, "black pride" ("race") or pride in being Italian or Irish (ethnicity), or pride in the customs of traditions of their family and heritage (culture).

Now that we know that there is no such thing as a race, how should we think about race? Should we think of "racial" categories as ethic or cultural groups? Should we continue to act as if "racial" differences are real?

What do you think? What questions do you have?

Part Two – Learning Guide for Charting a Course Beyond Racism TEDx Talk[6]

Summary of the TEDx Talk

In his TEDx talk (presented in Waltham MA by Carlos Hoyt on June 12, 2021), Hoyt draws on a personal anecdote to illuminate the flawed understanding and navigation of race in society. Hoyt likens societal navigation of race to being given incorrect directions that do not match the real-world terrain, emphasizing the need to reorient our understanding of race to truly move beyond racism.

<u>*Key Points:*</u>
- Hoyt critiques the concept of racial equality as contradictory since race itself is a construct designed to signify and perpetuate inequality.

- Through the analogy of selecting, sorting, and attributing characteristics based on superficial differences (demonstrated with jars of sugar and salt), Hoyt reveals how these mental processes contribute to racialization and the perpetuation of racism.
- Hoyt underscores that racialization – the process by which societies construct races as real, different, and unequal – serves as the foundation of racism.
- He challenges the audience to reexamine and reject the false cartography of human difference, advocating for a worldview that disclaims the concept of race entirely.

Explanation of "Racialization"

Racialization is the process of imposing racial identities on individuals or groups based on perceived physical or cultural differences, thus creating an artificial division among people. In the context of Hoyt's talk, racialization is recognized as the fundamental mechanism through which racism is created and sustained. Hoyt's usage emphasizes that racialization not only categorizes people into arbitrary groups based on superficial traits but also assigns value and hierarchical status to these groups, perpetuating systemic inequalities.

"Charting a Course Beyond Racism" serves as a call to reexamine and ultimately reject the deeply ingrained societally drawn maps of human difference which fail to match the realities of what makes us similar or dissimilar. By relinquishing the erroneous map and embracing a corrected orientation – one that recognizes the unity and equality of all human beings – we can begin the journey toward a truly inclusive and equitable world.

Transcript – Content of slides displayed during the talk appear in the form: "Slide: content."

When I was younger, I worked at a wonderful summer camp on beautiful Lake Thompson in West Poland, Maine. On many a day, my friends and I looked across the lake at a beautiful green meadow on a hillside in the near distance, and we wanted to go there.

On one of our days off, we set out to do just that. We figured it couldn't involve more than 15–20 minutes tops.

Well, over an hour into our precious 24 hours off, we were lost, frustrated, and desperate enough to ask for help.

We stopped at a small grocery/coffee/pizza/sub/deli/soft-serve ice cream/bait and tackle/guns and ammo/foreign auto repair/real estate office/laundromat/and gas station to ask for directions, and were told by the warm, suspendered, and plain-speaking proprietor, "Ayuh, that's Johnson Hill. You can't get there from here."

While this response felt more like an indictment than a pointer, it was meant to make us aware that the ROUTE we had in mind didn't match the actual terrain we needed to navigate.

The directions we got from our wise Maine guide didn't remotely match the roadmap we had in mind, but the map we had in mind didn't remotely match the real world.

ONCE WE REORIENTED ourselves to the corrected view of things, and followed our guide's direction, we were in fact able to arrive at our desired destination and enjoy the beautiful meadow on Johnson Hill.

Today, like the helpful Maine guide, I want to reorient the way we think about race.

To correct the bad roadmaps we have in our heads about race and provide directions that can actually lead us truly and finally beyond racism.

The map you likely have in your head about race tells you that to get beyond racism, we have to somehow arrive at RACIAL EQUALITY.

But the idea of racial equality is an oxymoron, an idea that contradicts itself. Like jumbo shrimp. Race is, by definition, about inequality. Race was invented to separate human beings on the false basis of unequal capacity and worth.

What I've learned standing and living at the intersection of my identities – as an immigrant, a male-socialized person, a child of poverty, and an upper-middle-class adult, as a father, and husband, as a teacher, a social worker, a psychotherapist, and as an adversely racialized person is that we haven't gotten beyond racism because we've been using the map of human differences and similarities CREATED BY THE RACISTS. Audre Lorde famously said the master's tools will never destroy the master's house.

In the spirit of Lorde's insight, we need to see that the master's map will never take us beyond the master's boundaries – the false boundaries of human difference created to keep us on one side or the other of social advantage or social disadvantage.

The master's map is a product of the process of racialization, the process by which we literally create races, which in turn serve as the basis and justification for racism.

We haven't succeeded in overcoming racism – in fact, many might say things are almost as bad as ever – because we are using the master's false cartography of human difference as our guide – because we persist in racializing others and ourselves.

I'm going to provide some directions – some corrective road signs – and take us on a journey away from the misunderstandings we have about race so that we can truly and finally get beyond racism.

Before we start our journey away from racism, let's take a vision screening test to make sure we're fit to drive.

Figure 2.7 The Three Jars

What do you see?
Which jars contain substances that are most alike?

Jars 1 and 2?
Jars 1 and 3?
Jars 2 and 3?

On what evidence or basis are you making your decisions?

It turns out that Jar 1 contains white sugar. Jar 2 contains brown sugar. Jar 3 contains salt

Now that you know what's actually in each jar, which jars contain the substances that are most alike?

What's the difference between white sugar and brown sugar?

It's just one thing.

MOLASSES

Slide: What a fool believes, they see.

If you're like most people who do this activity, you just experienced a couple of feelings: cognitive dissonance – that feeling you get when the world tells you that what you thought was right is wrong and foolishness – that "Oh, how stupid of me to be so easily fooled!" feeling.

If you felt a little fooled, that's OK – as long as we learn from our mistakes, right?

So, what's the lesson?

Well, one way to state lesson might be: It's stupid to draw conclusions based on meagre and superficial information. Don't be stupid.

But that's a little harsh. It's true, but we can go deeper into this lesson. We can learn what causes us to make this kind of mistake.

You made the mistake about the jars because your brain was doing what brains do – thinking fast and making assumptions that then serve as the basis for actions.

Here are the steps your brain took when I presented the three jars and asked which two were most alike.

It's a pretty simple but highly consequential five-step process.

1. First, your brain SELECTED some noticeable superficial characteristics of the substances that could serve as the basis for differentiation and categorization. We are categorizing machines.

Your brain selected color (and possibly texture) as a clear distinguishing characteristic. *Two of these things are the same color. One of these things is a different color from the other two.*

2. Next, your brain SORTED the substances based on similarity or dissimilarity of the selection criteria, color.

White substances over here; brown substances over there.

3. At step number three, things start to get really interesting.

THE NEXT THING YOUR BRAIN DOES IS GO BEYOND WHAT IT SEES TO DEVELOP BELIEFS ABOUT WHAT IT CANNOT SEE.

We are speculation machines.

Your brain ATTRIBUTED or assigned similar underlying qualities to things that appear similar on the surface.

These white substances look alike; therefore, they are alike in other ways. If I could feel them, they'd feel the same. If I could taste them, they would taste the same because they are the same. *The things that are the same color share underlying qualities not shared with the thing that is a different color.*

Once your flawed mapping was corrected, you were able to understand the substances in a way that actually aligned with reality – and you made the correction pretty easily.

When the course correction is about something we don't have a strong attachment to, we tend to be able to adjust without too much trouble, stress, or resistance.

As the stakes get higher and your convictions and conditioning get stronger and deeper, however, it can be harder to let go of our preconceived maps of the world.

Figure 2.8 Carlos Hoyt and Evan Hoyt

What do you see?
What's different about these two people?
What's alike about these two people?
What's the relationship between these two people?
HINT: What did we learn from the three jars?

SELECTING, SORTING, ATTRIBUTING, ESSENTIALIZING
The person on the left is yours truly.
The person on the right is Evan Carlos Hoyt.
Evan Carlos Hoyt is my son.
I made him. By which I mean I played a small part in making him with his mom, my wife, Leslie.
If you allow yourself to see past the master's cartography of difference, you'll see that Evan and I actually share several craniofacial features.
He's on the way to having his dad's eyebrows.
Our eyes are the same shape.
Same with our nose, ears, mouth, chin, and jawline.
We even have freckles in common.

What stopped you from seeing all that I have in common with my son right away?

What's the difference between dark skin and light skin?

Just one thing.

Melanin.

When we apply the process of SELECTING, SORTING, ATTRIBUTING, ESSENTIALIZING, ACTING to the way we see and treat human beings, we are performing the process of racialization – creating the false construction of race within which we are all trapped and lost.

Here's what your brain does on racialization:

I quote:

Anyone who thinks that white and black people look as different as we do on the outside, but are somehow magically the same on the inside, is delusional. How could our faces, skin, hair, and body structure all be different, but our brains be exactly the same?

This articulation of racialization comes from Dylann Roof, who massacred nine black-racialized people in a Church in Charleston, South Carolina, on June 17, 2015.

Roof's racialization process led to terrible, evil, lethal action.

I said, here's what YOUR brain does on racialization, and then I read the words of one of the most vicious and murderous racists in US history.

Please know I meant no offense by putting you in the same category as a vile and unrepentant racist and mass murderer. I do not think any of you are MEAN and EVIL racists.

I'm sure each of you is a very KIND racist. Like doctors, who are clearly fine, kind people who believe in treating people equally and doing no harm.

Yet half of all white-identified medical trainees and interns believe that black-racialized people's skin is thicker than white-racialized people's.

When you see families like mine.

When you decide what neighborhood you'll live in, who you'll date, marry, and have children with, what schools those children will go to, who you'll vote for, march for, die for.

All these decisions about how to ACT stemming from the racialization process – no matter your best intentions and best effort to be ANTIRACIST and bring about racial equality – will only ever end up reifying, recapitulating, and reinforcing the very essence of racism.

If you truly want to be anti-racist – as so many people seem to want to be these days – you're going to have to learn to be *anti-racialization*.

If we truly want to get beyond racism, we're going to have to stop seeing and navigating the world according to the master's false and devious CARTOGRAPHY of human differences.

Using that bad map only keeps us stuck in a terrible rotary.

Trying to drive away from racism while maintaining the BASIS of racism.

We intend to drive away from something and end up where we started.

And we've been going around and around ever since – driving while racialized – hoping to get beyond racism while reproducing the very thing that makes racism INEVITABLE.

Before we knew better, this mistake was understandable. We were doing the best we could under the circumstances.

Instead of DISCLAIMING – REJECTING ALTOGETHER the idea of race when it started to become a way to understand and navigate human differences – we made noble but misguided efforts to RECLAIM it.

But we've known better for quite some time now that the idea of race is not only absurd; it's lethally absurd.

And yet we keep behaving as if race is every bit as real as we thought it was when we didn't know better.

We broke the shackle on the body but left the shackle of the mind intact.

Is it too late to adjust to the accurate maps of human differences and similarity and solidarity? Has the shackle of the mind become unbreakable?

No. I can give you proof that it's not too late.

I offer myself.

I am NOT a racist.

And I realize I'm saying that at a time when it is almost expected that everyone needs to confess to being a racist.

I am NOT a racist.

And I'm not a racist based on advocating COLORBLINDNESS or claiming that we've crossed into a POST-RACE era.

We're still quite stuck on the race rotary.

I'm not a racist because I know better than to believe in a false construction of human difference that only serves to separate people into superior and subjugated.

I'm not a racist because I understand the process of racialization, and I dedicate my life to working against the peril of racism that racialization produces.

And I can introduce you to others who have found the exit ramp out of the race rotary.

If you'd like to join us, here are four directions for getting out of the race rotary and moving beyond racism.

Slide: Be aware of your racialization habit.

Knowing you have a problem is crucial to solving your problem.
Slide: Stop referring to people as members of categories that don't exist.
Slide: Start recognizing people not as *races* but as *racialized*.
Slide: Understand that racialization is the source of race and racism, and resist it mightily.
Slide: We get where we get when we get there.

Being a therapist, I know and honor that people get where they get when they get there.

As a therapist, I know that a critical step in helping many folks heal and grow is to help them abandon fundamentally false constructions of their world that keep them stuck and suffering.

But such work takes time. It's not a "snap out of it" process.

Directions aren't dictums. We could have ignored our wise Maine guide and NEVER have gotten to that green meadow.

It can take a while to come around to seeing things differently.

It took a while for us to stop thinking and acting as if the Earth is flat.

It took a while for us to stop believing and acting as if the Earth is the center of what we now know is our SOLAR system.

It's taking a while to end our misguided attachment to race.

We get where we get when we get there.

That's a tautology – an undeniable truth.

Here's another one regarding getting past racism while continuing to practice racialization:

We won't get there from here.

We can't get there using the master's map.

BUT we can get there if we REORIENT TO A BETTER MAP.

Slide: Ready to use a better map?

Part Three – The Three Jars Lesson Procedure for Young Learners

1. If you have an actual version of the three jars or perhaps several of them (which you can make by simply fastening the jars with an adhesive that bonds glass surfaces, labeling them 1, 2, and 3, and filling them with white sugar, brown sugar, and salt respectively), pass them around, and give each child a chance to give them a careful look.

    If you do not have actual jars, use an image of the jars (such as the one later). Also be prepared to provide an image of Carlos and his son Evan later in the exercise.

2. Tell the children that after we look at the jars silently – just using our eyes and brains to learn about them – you're going to ask them some questions about them.

3. If any child is unable to see the jars, describe them in as much detail as possible, emphasizing that they are exactly alike except for the numbers and the stuff inside them.
4. After the children have had ample time to develop thoughts about what they are seeing when they look at the jars, go through the series of questions and prompts later in the order presented.
5. As the students share their perceptions, observe that different brains seeing or thinking about the same thing can have different thoughts (diversity of brains and ideas!), praise them for noticing so many details and for thinking so well about why they see things the way they do.
6. When the exercise is completed, ask the students how they might teach the lesson to others (e.g., their siblings or parents or other teachers or the school head). If any students want to try this at home, invite them to draw a version of the three jars to use in their lesson. You might also consider having color images of the jars that students can take home with them.

Figure 2.9 The Three Jars

Questions and Prompts
1. What do you see?
2. Which jars contain substances that are most alike?
3. Jars 1 and 2?
4. Jars 1 and 3?
5. Jars 2 and 3?
6. On what evidence or basis are you making your decisions?
7. It turns out that Jar 1 contains white sugar. Jar 2 contains brown sugar. Jar 3 contains salt
8. Now that you know what's actually in each jar, which jars contain the substances that are most alike?
9. What's the difference between white sugar and brown sugar?
10. It's just one thing.
11. MOLASSES
12. What do you see?
13. What's different about these two people?
14. What's alike about these two people?
15. What's the relationship between these two people?
16. Hɪɴᴛ: What did we learn from the three jars?

Figure 2.10 Carlos Hoyt and Evan Hoyt

17. The person on the left is Carlos Hoyt.
18. The person on the right is Evan Carlos Hoyt.
19. Evan Carlos Hoyt is Carlos Hoyt's son.
20. What do you think made it hard to see that Carlos and Evan are father and son?
21. If you look at the two of them closely, you can see that:
22. Evan is on his way to having his dad's eyebrows.
23. Evan and Carlos's eyes are the same shape.
24. That's also true for their noses, ears, mouths, chins, and jawlines.
25. They even have freckles in common. Carlos's are just a little hard to see because of his dark skin.
26. What stopped you from seeing all that Carlos and Evan have in common right away?
27. Do you remember what the difference is between dark or brown sugar and light or white sugar?
28. It's just one thing: molasses.
29. What's the difference between dark skin and light skin?
30. Just one thing.
31. Melanin.
32. What did we learn?

Touchstone/Tool #9: Gauging Belonging: The Student Belonging Feedback Channel

The Student Belonging Feedback Channel is an innovative approach for educational institutions committed to inclusivity to continually assess and improve the sense of belonging among students. This guide explains the Channel and on how schools can operationalize this commitment through its use. The Channel is presented as an example of a model that uses data (in this case, qualitative data) to go beyond impressions and anecdotes as methods for determining if antibias efforts are effective. The purpose of offering it is not to prescribe it as something that must be used as presented or at all. The point is to support DEI educators in thinking about how they can use this model or develop and implement something different – but one way or another, find ways to bring data to bear on DEI practices.

Implementation of Student Belonging Feedback Channel

Step 1: Establish the Channel
- Create a Safe and Accessible Platform: This can be an online portal, a physical suggestion box, or regular in-person forums where students can share feedback anonymously if they choose.
- Communicate Purpose Clearly: Make sure students understand that this channel is specifically designed for them to express how school policies, practices, and everyday interactions affect their sense of belonging.
- Establish the Role of Belonging Channel Facilitator: A person who will receive Thriving and Striving reports, and support students and teachers in connecting to discuss the content of reports.

Step 2: Encourage Feedback
- Promote the Channel: Regularly remind students of the feedback channel through school announcements, posters, and during classes.
- Educate on Feedback Types: Clarify the difference between 'Thriving' feedback (positive experiences) and 'Striving' feedback (areas for improvement).

Step 3: Provide Assurance
- Ensure Responsiveness: Set a clear protocol that all feedback will be read, and 'Striving' feedback will receive a response or acknowledgment within a specified timeframe.

- Take Action: Demonstrate that feedback leads to action. Publicize changes or initiatives taken in response to student feedback.

Step 4: Multiple Methods for Providing Input
In addition to the Student Belonging Feedback Channel, schools should offer other opportunities to provide feedback:
- Schedule Regular Check-Ins: Create opportunities for students to discuss feedback and suggest improvements in an open forum (e.g., homeroom groups or advisory groups).
- Offer Reflective Sessions: Periodically hold sessions where students can reflect on how the school's actions have impacted their sense of belonging.
- Anonymous Surveys and Assessments: Regularly distribute anonymous surveys that measure students' sense of belonging and perceptions of the school's inclusivity.

Step 5: Are We Helping, and How Do We Know? Evaluating Impact
- Assess Changes: Regularly evaluate the effectiveness of changes made in response to feedback.
- Discern Patterns: Examine indicators of improvement and room for improvement within and across all input methods.
- Qualitative Data: Include impressions and anecdotes from teachers, students, and parents as additional forms of useful data.
- Stakeholder Meetings: Include teachers, parents, and students in discussions about feedback results and the school's inclusivity efforts.
- Reporting Back: Share with the school community how feedback is being used to improve the school environment.

Step 6: Partnering with Parents on the Student Belonging Feedback Channel
Effective implementation of the Student Belonging Feedback Channel extends beyond the classroom and involves a partnership with parents. Clear communication with parents about the existence and purpose of the Channel is crucial. Here are steps to ensure parents are informed and engaged:

Informing Parents:
- Introduce the Feedback Channel during parent-teacher meetings, school newsletters, or dedicated communication from the school administration.
- Explain how the Channel supports student well-being, inclusivity, and belonging.

Engaging Parents:
- Encourage parents to discuss the Feedback Channel with their children, emphasizing its role as a supportive tool for student expression.
- Invite parents to share their observations or conversations with their children that might provide valuable feedback through the Channel.

Empowering Younger Students Through Parents:
- Acknowledge that younger students may not be able to articulate their experiences directly through the Channel.
- Encourage parents of younger students to act on their child's behalf, providing an avenue for their feedback to be heard.

Parental Feedback Submission:
- Offer clear instructions on how parents can submit feedback, either thriving or striving, to the Channel staff facilitator or other designated school staff.
- Ensure parents understand that their submissions are valued and will be addressed with the same consideration as feedback coming directly from students.

Building Trust:
- Reassure parents that the school is committed to creating a safe and supportive environment where all feedback is used constructively.
- Emphasize the confidentiality and respect with which feedback from parents and students will be treated.

Collaborative Follow-Up:
- Establish a system for following up on feedback received from parents, keeping them informed of any steps taken as a result of their communication.
- Where appropriate, involve parents in the process of addressing the feedback, fostering a cooperative approach to enhancing the school environment.

By engaging parents as allies in the Student Belonging Feedback Channel, schools can foster a more comprehensive and community-oriented approach to student well-being and inclusivity. This collaborative effort ensures that the voices of all students, especially those who may feel less empowered to speak up, are heard and addressed, reinforcing the school's commitment to care and support for every student.

By thoughtfully implementing and maintaining the Student Belonging Feedback Channel, schools demonstrate a concrete commitment to inclusivity.

This system allows schools to remain agile in their responses to the evolving needs and concerns of their student body, ensuring that they are not only helping but consistently seeking to improve the educational environment.

Why the Channel Is Not Anonymous

The value of the channel turns on (1) trust that there will be no negative reactions to students' honest and constructive feedback, (2) a goal of building students' sense of entitlement to express themselves civilly and constructively, and (3) the use of the channel to connect students and adults to celebrate thriving situations and work through striving situations. Only through these aspects of the model can a trained and trusted adult be able to monitor data and, most importantly, help students and teachers continually improve inclusivity at their school.

By adhering to these guidelines, schools can make the Student Belonging Feedback Channel a vital tool for building an inclusive school culture where every student feels valued and heard.

Sample Note to Teachers about the Student Belonging Feedback Channel

Dear Teachers,

Your commitment to nurturing and educating your students is what shapes the future one classroom at a time. We recognize that part of this journey includes receiving feedback that may not always reflect our intentions. It's natural to feel a bit anxious about receiving striving reports – after all, they can sometimes feel like reflections of our shortcomings. It's entirely natural for teachers to experience a sense of apprehension at the prospect of receiving striving reports through the Student Belonging Feedback Channel. The dedication teachers have to their students' well-being and educational experience often means that any indication of falling short of these goals can be a source of concern. However, it's important to reframe and embrace the feedback channel not as a critique of their efforts, but as an additional means of communication that benefits students who might find it more comfortable to express their thoughts in this manner.

Yet, it's crucial to remember that these reports are not about judging your competence or care; they are about communication. Students express themselves in different ways, and the Student Belonging Feedback Channel provides them with a platform to voice their experiences in a manner that might feel safe and accessible to them.

When you receive a striving report, it's an opportunity – a sign that a student trusts the system enough to reach out and share their perspective.

It's a courageous step for a student to take, and it speaks to the trust they place in us as educators to listen and respond with empathy and action.

The feedback channel is a means to bridge communication gaps, providing an accessible avenue for students who may not yet have the confidence or the means to express themselves directly. It serves as a crucial equity measure, ensuring that all students, irrespective of their confidence levels, trust in authority, or social capital, have the opportunity to be seen and heard.

For students, particularly those who might feel marginalized or less empowered to speak up, the channel offers a voice. It empowers them to share their experiences in a structured and safe manner, and it assures them that their perspectives are valued and critical to the school's commitment to inclusivity and care.

For teachers, this feedback is an extension of the classroom conversation. It is an important barometer that can signal when a student needs more support or when classroom dynamics may need adjusting. The feedback provided through the channel can often illuminate issues that might not be immediately visible in the day-to-day interactions of a busy classroom.

Here's how teachers can embrace the Student Belonging Feedback Channel:

Acknowledge Your Feelings: It's okay to feel apprehensive. Acknowledge this feeling as a sign of your investment in your students' success and happiness.

Approach with Curiosity: Instead of apprehension, try to approach the feedback with curiosity. What can this teach you about your student's needs? How can this improve your teaching practice?

Respond with Gratitude: Thank the student for their feedback. It's a valuable insight into their experience and an essential tool for your professional growth.

See the Bigger Picture: Every Striving report is a piece of a larger puzzle. It contributes to a more comprehensive understanding of your classroom dynamics and helps create a more inclusive and supportive learning environment.

View the Channel as a Supportive Tool:
- Understand that feedback, even when it highlights areas for improvement, is a form of support and guidance from students.
- Acknowledge that the channel provides insights into student well-being and can be instrumental in fostering a supportive learning environment.
- Recognize the Channel as an important form of empowerment and equity that provides a safe and constructive means for all students to share important feelings and perceptions and connect with their teachers.

Normalize the Reception of Feedback:
- Regularly discuss the value of feedback in personal and professional growth, normalizing it as part of the school culture.
- Share experiences of how feedback has been beneficial in the past, demonstrating its positive outcomes.

Maintain an Open Dialogue:
- Encourage students to use the channel by creating an atmosphere of open dialogue and by expressing a genuine willingness to listen and adapt.
- Address feedback openly where appropriate, showing that it is taken seriously and acted upon.

Supportive Actions:
- Discuss the feedback with a trusted colleague or mentor for a different perspective and support.
- Attend workshops or training on DEI and communication to build skills in responding to and learning from feedback.

Reflect and Act:
- Reflect on the feedback received, discussing with colleagues or mentors to gain perspective and ideas for constructive responses.
- Develop an action plan based on the feedback, showing students that their input leads to tangible changes.

By embracing the feedback channel as a means to facilitate communication, we open up new pathways to connect with our students and better understand their needs. Let's welcome this opportunity to enhance our teaching and foster a community where every student feels they belong.

Thank you for your constant dedication to educating and caring for our students. We are all lucky to have you!

Sincerely,

[Principal/Head of School]

Sample Letter to Parents about the Student Belonging Feedback Channel

Subject: Partnering Together for Student Growth and Inclusivity: Introducing the Student Belonging Feedback Channel

Dear Parents and Guardians,

I hope this message finds you well and embracing the vibrancy of the new school year. We are writing to you with a shared vision – a vision that every student in our care feels valued, understood, and integral to our school community. To bring this vision to life, we are excited to introduce the Student Belonging Feedback Channel, an innovative approach to nurturing a culture of belonging and inclusivity.

What is the Student Belonging Feedback Channel?

The Feedback Channel is a proactive communication tool designed to give students a voice, allowing them to share feedback directly with school staff regarding their experiences of belonging – celebrating positive instances ("Thriving Feedback") and addressing areas for growth ("Striving Feedback"). It is a platform based on trust, openness, and our collective commitment to the well-being of our students.

Why a Feedback Channel?

We understand that communication is multifaceted. While some students feel comfortable speaking up in person, others may prefer a different approach to express their thoughts. The Feedback Channel ensures that all students, regardless of their age, background, or confidence level, have an equal opportunity to be heard.[7]

Your Role as Parents

As parents, you play an irreplaceable role in your child's education. Your insights into your child's feelings and school experiences are invaluable. We encourage you to discuss the Feedback Channel with your child and use it as a springboard for conversations about their school life.

For parents of younger students or those who may need assistance, please know that your voice is equally important. If your child has something to share but is not ready to use the Channel, we warmly invite you to convey feedback on their behalf.

How Can You Participate?

Engage in Dialogue: Talk with your child about their day-to-day school experiences and the importance of sharing their thoughts to contribute to a positive school environment.

Submit Feedback: If your child has feedback they would like to share, or if you have observations as a parent, please reach out to the Channel staff facilitator or any staff member to communicate this feedback.

Trust in Confidentiality: Rest assured that all feedback is treated with the utmost confidentiality and respect, and it will be used constructively to enhance our students' school experience.

Expect Follow-Up: We are committed to following up on all feedback – whether it's recognizing a teacher's effort that has made your child feel particularly welcome or addressing a concern that impacts your child's sense of belonging.

Next Steps

In the coming days, we will provide more detailed information about the Student Belonging Feedback Channel through our school's portal, including guidelines and how to submit feedback. We will also be hosting a virtual parent information session next month to discuss this initiative further and answer any questions you may have.

Closing Thoughts

We believe that open communication and partnership with families are key to creating an educational environment where every student can thrive. Your involvement is not just welcomed – it is essential for the success of this initiative.

Together, let's ensure that our school continues to be a place where every student's voice is heard and valued.

Warm regards,

[Signatures]

Sample Slides for Introducing and Explaining the Student Belonging Feedback Channel

Slide 1: The Student Belonging Feedback Channel – A virtuous feedback loop for students and teachers

Slide 2: What is Belonging

Belonging is defined as a unique and subjective experience that relates to a yearning for connection with others, the need for positive regard, and the desire for interpersonal connection.

A sense of belonging has been described as a fundamental human motivation underpinned by a pervasive and compelling need to belong that we continually seek to find and maintain.

Even as we strive to belong, we are also deeply conditioned to provide a sense of belonging to others.

It is our sense of belonging and its importance to us as a species that shapes the way our relationships with others, groups, and even how whole communities, function.

An absence of belonging has negative and devastating effects on people, both physically and psychologically.

Slide 3: Our community

Every day at school there are countless instances of affirmation of belonging, empowerment, and our commitment to honor differences and live by our school values.

Because there are no perfect humans, it's possible that sometimes a student might feel confused or upset by something done by an adult at school.

Slide 4: Everyone is capable of displaying biases they might not even be aware of. This is especially true when we are interacting with people who are from backgrounds we don't know a lot about.

Bias – Leaning towards something and away from something else [consider inserting an image of the Leaning Tower of Pisa here]

Slide 5: The Social Identity Prism helps us understand how bias happens [insert the Social Identity Prism on this slide]

Slide 6: Every adult at school wants to know if they do anything that causes you to feel less than fully welcome, seen, heard, empowered, valued, and embraced

No adult at school will ever get mad or make you feel bad if you let them know that something they did made you feel uncomfortable or upset. Instead, they'll be proud of you and grateful – and they will do everything they can to make things better.

Slide 7: Providing Space to Share

Ideally, every student, no matter their age or social identity, should feel safe and empowered to talk directly with the adults in their lives about everything, including behaviors that make them feel uncomfortable.

We recognize, however, that sometimes differences in status, power, and backgrounds and the length and nature of a relationship can stand in the way of feeling safe enough to speak up.

Slide 8: We know teachers want to help students feel safe and welcome

And we know sometimes it is hard to give feedback.

The Student Feedback Channel is an easy way for students to give that feedback. Teachers really do want to be informed, so use it!

Slide 9: The Student Belonging Feedback Channel

Provides a safe and constant method for you to do two extremely important things about your sense of belonging at school

Thriving: Letting your teachers know when they do something that makes you feel known, respected, empowered, and happy at school.

Striving: Letting your teachers know when they do something that makes you feel uncomfortable or upset.

Slide 10: Student Belonging Feedback Channel – A User's Guide

Slide 11: [On this slide you should present the instruction for students (and parents of younger children) to access the Feedback Channel Survey

Slide 12: Kindness should never silence Justice

Sometimes people hesitate to say something that is critical of another person's behavior.

Speaking up for ourselves can seem to be in conflict with being a nice/kind person.

We want you to practice the skill of being able to seek justice in a kind and compassionate way.

Sometimes speaking up might involve someone feeling a little bad about their behavior.

You might feel a little bad about sharing your thoughts.

That's okay.

Sharing your thoughts helps others become aware of the problem so they can fix it!

Slide 13: Stating negative impact AND assuming positive intent

We can express concerns about another person's behavior AND have faith that . . .

The person is not seeking to harm us, and the person wishes to correct any behaviors that are harmful to us.

Slide 14: People are people, and behavior is behavior

People are not reducible to any behavior they commit. When we provide feedback, focus on the behavior, not on negative assumptions about the person.

Don't focus on the person: My teacher is insensitive and must not care about me because they divide students into "boys" and "girls" groups, which makes me feel unseen and disrespected because I don't define my gender the way most people assume I would.

Do focus on behavior: When my teacher divides the students into "boys" and "girls" groups, it makes me feel unseen and disrespected because I don't define my gender the way most people assume I would.

Slide 15: What Happens to your Thriving or Striving Feedback

On this slide include clear information about who will receive the reports and how they will engage with the student and teacher to facilitate constructive interaction.

Slide 16: To recap . . .

On this slide include any summary information you think would be useful for your students.

Touchstone/Tool #10: Learning Outcomes and Competencies for All Students – The Diversity Without Divisiveness Antibias Standards

A DEI curriculum must enumerate the key knowledge that students should be able to acquire as a result of instruction/facilitation. As with any content area, DEI teaching and learning should be grounded in a set of anchor standards and learning outcomes. The Diversity Without Divisiveness (DWD) Antibias Standards provide a foundational framework for DEI education, focusing on developing knowledges necessary to successfully navigate an increasingly diverse and interconnected world.

The DWD Antibias Standards are divided into six domains – Identity, Diversity, Equity, Inclusivity, Human Psychology, and DEI Choices. The standards emphasize scholarship, learning factual information, and critical thinking skills. The standards do not presume to prescribe values, worldviews, ideologies, or political stances. Instead, they provide a clear and accessible framework within which every student can synthesize their own bearing on the subject matter. Unlike similar standards that prescribe attitudinal and behavioral outcomes, the DWD Antibias Standards emphasize the primacy of each individual's right to exercise their agency in determining what to do with what they learn.

The standards provide a common language and organizational structure that teachers can use to develop age-appropriate curricula, and administrators can use to make schools more safe, equitable, inclusive, and productive. The standards should be considered starting points and can be adapted as necessary to meet the needs of different educational settings.

The DWD Antibias Standards are not a fully detailed scope and sequence. Instead, the six anchor standards and learning outcomes are organized from basic to more complex, with the first few standards in each domain being appropriate for early and elementary grades. Teaching that centers on identity and diversity are the foundation for later concepts and should be taught first.

Parts Two and Three of the book provide some guidance, lessons, and resources that pertain to these standards. However, ultimate instructional decisions are left to the practitioner and the school so that lessons and resources educators create will reflect the needs and goals of their unique circumstances.

Diversity Without Divisiveness Antibias Standards

Identity
1. Students will understand the meaning of the concept of identity
2. Students will understand the difference and the interaction between personal and social identity

3. Students will understand the primary social identity categories and how they interact to form complex individuals
4. Students will understand that identity often serves as the basis of pride, belonging, and solidarity with others who share one's identity.
5. Students will understand that identity often serves as the basis for excluding those who do not share one's identity.
6. Students will understand the differences between scientific, empirical methods of categorizing human differences and social customs of group categorization

Diversity
1. Students will understand that diversity is inherent and essential to all forms of life, including human beings
2. Students will understand that there are macro-commonalities (across groups), mezzo-commonalities (within groups), and micro qualities (individual uniqueness) within the human species
3. Students will understand the benefits of diversity when effective equity and inclusivity are in place, and how diversity can result in conflict when effective equity and inclusivity measures are not in place

Equity
1. Students will understand that equity means everyone getting what they need to have equal opportunities, not everyone getting the same thing or achieving the same outcomes
2. Students will understand inequitable treatment associated with each primary social identity group
3. Students will understand how social bias operates
4. Students will understand how laws, policies, and practices are designed to create equity and social justice with varying degrees of expansivist or restrictivist outcomes

Inclusivity
1. Students will understand that inclusivity means everyone being welcomed, respected, valued, and represented in their communities, resulting in a sense of belonging
2. Students will understand methods for assessing a sense of inclusivity/belonging

Human Psychology
1. Students will understand the concept and application of empathy as crucial in understanding behavioral differences that might be associated with social identity and social bias

2. Students will understand how socialization shapes a person's views, values, and choices regarding social identity, social bias, and social justice issues
3. Students will understand the important differences and tension between private belief and public tolerance
4. Students will understand the social bias concepts of prejudice, stereotyping, racialization, and the specific forms of bias ("isms") associated with each primary social identity category
5. Students will understand how to apply critical thinking to challenging situations and dynamics associated with diversity, equity, and inclusivity and social identity, social bias, and social justice

Elaboration on Each DWD Antibias Standard

Identity

Understanding identity is foundational in helping children recognize and appreciate both their uniqueness and their connections to others.

Identity begins with simple concepts for young children such as their names or favorite things. As they grow, children see themselves both as individuals and members of various groups.

The simplest definition of identity centers on who and what a child is. Young children will start very concretely and give their name as who they are. They will list their likes, "My favorite color is . . .", and their dislikes, "I do not like tuna fish." This can be explored in concrete activities such as looking in a mirror and creating self-portraits, making collage identity silhouettes, or filling in identity wheels.

Young children tend to recognize their personal identity through many dimensions. They use their physical characteristics (I'm the tallest in the class), their abilities (I'm the fastest runner), their function (I'm the line leader) or their likes (I'm a Swiftie) or dislikes to describe who they are. This then becomes their personal identity at that moment.

Beyond an individual's self-perception, social identity has to do with the groups that one is a part of. This could include one's family or school. This could also include the groups that people assume you are a member of. One's personal and group identity can overlap and be the same; however, they may not always coincide.

Social identity can include categories such as race, gender, ethnicity, sexual orientation. For instance, a child may identify as a "big sister" (personal identity) and also as part of a family or a team (social identity). Both kinds of identity – personal identity and social identity – are important because they help us understand who we are as individuals and how we fit into the bigger picture with others. It's like knowing your own puzzle piece and seeing how it fits into a giant puzzle with everyone else's pieces.

The Social Identity Prism creates a visual representation of the multiple social identities that can encompass an individual. They include ability, age, family-ethnicity-heritage, gender, physical appearance, racialization, sexual orientation, social status, worldview/ideology and the "+" category meant which is meant to acknowledge any other social identity that is important to a person.

Depending on age and content areas, these identities can be explored through discussions, activities, literature, and current events. For example, a unit on voting rights would involve an exploration of many of these social identities and lends itself to the examination of the intersection of power and social identity.

As students explore identity and begin to share parts of themselves in a group, they will begin to recognize similarities, differences, and connections. They will appreciate the complexity of their own personal and social identities as well as the identities of their peers.

In early childhood classes, literature as well as social stories can illustrate instances of exclusion and belonging based on social identities. Connections can be made to history where social identities often serve as the basis for exclusion, oppression, and war.

Lessons on human differences can be grounded in science and made developmentally appropriate for even young learners. For example, the Three Jars Exercise about race can be taught as young as nursery-aged children. Older students can learn about DNA and genetic characteristics in life science courses or units.

Clear and explicit lessons on identity enable students to better understand who they are, how they connect with others, and who others are – skills crucial for personal development and social interaction.

Diversity

A concrete and very basic way to illustrate the benefits of diversity is to show the benefits of having choices and options. It is much more fun, exciting, interesting to have many different color markers than to have just one color. It can be more compelling and engaging to use more than one type of media to create artwork. And not just many different colors of markers but many different types of markers, and markers and crayons and pastels and paints can create depth and perspective. Just as using a variety of art media can enhance a piece of artwork, incorporating diverse perspectives and experiences enriches group projects and classroom discussions, promoting a more vibrant and inclusive learning environment.

As part of teaching the complexity of identity and diversity, students will understand their relationship to different groups. Diversity encompasses various dimensions – micro, mezzo, and macro – that affect our personal identities, social interactions, and the broader social justice landscape. The "micro" level focuses on individual characteristics, the "mezzo" level on group affiliations within communities like schools or cities, and the "macro" level on larger societal constructs. A simple illustration of these concepts could be your micro identity is your first name, your mezzo could be your last name that signifies the family that you belong to and your kin that share that last name. The macro could be if you did a genetic test and found your ancestors and relatives that share your DNA from all over the world.

It would be naive to say that diversity does not have its challenges. It could be said that it is much easier to make dinner for a group that all had the same tastes. One could make one meal that was equally enjoyed by all. It is harder to meet the needs and tastes of a diverse group that has different preferences and unique dietary needs. A cook may need to make different variations of the same types of foods to make sure that everyone had a similar, enjoyable experience. The vegan entree would need to be as hearty as the meat entree. The positive end result could be a much more interesting meal where people are exposed to new types of food out of their usual repertoire and learn something new about themselves and others around them.

Failure to address diversity of backgrounds/needs can result in social bias which can play out on the micro, mezzo, and macro level. Social bias can be filtered through micro, mezzo, and macro dimensions as well. On the micro level, one can disagree with something because of their personal tastes or experiences they had. They might be biased against playing with others who look a certain way. On the mezzo level, a group could be biased against another group. The macro level bias is one of a larger scale involving social, structural, systemic, and institutional forces.

By continuously exploring and addressing the complexities of diversity, students are better prepared to build their knowledge and skills and apply this to historical and present conditions.

Equity

Equity means providing people with what they need so that they may experience life and liberty, and pursue happiness without having to contend with social bias or other forms of unfair disadvantage. Equality means providing everyone with the same things, regardless of their individual needs or circumstances.

Similar to the dinner example, students can grasp abstract concepts with concrete, relatable references. A pizza party that aims to be equitable will serve different types of pizza. The host may ask guests before the event what their preferences or dietary needs are. Everyone at the party may have a first slice before being able to take multiple slices. These practices are ensuring equity, and in this case the goal is to have everyone have access to a slice of pizza they can eat. They are not all having the same pizza, and they may not all eat the same amount, but everyone has what they need to take advantage of the opportunity to have a slice of pizza they can eat. In this example, pizza eaters may have different slices because of preferences, but they may need a certain type of pizza because of dietary needs.

Students can see how educational resources might be distributed based on student needs. Some students have special education services, whether it is small group instruction, one-on-one assistance, or access to certain tools such as speech-to-text programs. Equity practices can address other needs such as physical accessibility, language barriers, or learning differences.

Units and lessons that explicitly teach the "isms" can explore history through the lens of civil rights and laws that create access and equal protection regardless of social identities.

Younger children can learn about inequitable treatment through fictional picture books and autobiographies of famous individuals who overcame inequitable treatment based on their social identity group.

Social *bias* is *leaning* towards or away from a person or people because they are categorized as members of a social identity group. Social bias takes the form of privileging some social identity groups and discriminating against other social identity groups.

Even young children can understand the concept of likes/dislikes, preferences, and personal and social bias. Students can begin concretely with personal biases, and then examples can become more complex as students become older. The learning is then extended to social bias and how social bias can influence actions.

Equity means providing what individuals and groups need in order to have equal opportunity, security, health, education, and other social necessities. For example, some people need prescriptive eyeglasses to see. It would not make sense to say that everyone needs to wear eyeglasses or the same prescription of eyeglasses. Based on categories like age, ability, social status, and other factors, individuals will always need different resources to be fully and fairly included in society.

Students can learn about laws such as the Americans with Disabilities Act that strive to foster equity and inclusivity by ensuring accessibility. Equity, inclusivity, and accessibility are all closely aligned and to achieve any one of them, the others must be accounted for and taken into consideration.

For younger students or as a starting point for older students, classroom rules and expectations or school policies can be used to illustrate how equity and social justice can be established in an organization, institution, or classroom.

Students could also brainstorm responses to reflection questions such as the following:
1. How might understanding equity change the way you think about fairness in school settings?
2. Can you think of a time when you benefited from an equity-based approach?

Inclusivity

Inclusivity refers to the practice and policy of including people who might otherwise be excluded or marginalized. This includes ensuring all individuals, regardless of their diverse backgrounds, characteristics, or conditions, feel a sense of belonging, are welcomed, respected, and valued. An inclusive environment actively seeks to involve all community members, providing equal access to opportunities and resources while acknowledging and valuing the unique contributions each person can offer.

Concrete and natural conversations should happen at the beginning of each school year with a focus on defining and understanding the importance of a sense of belonging, feeling welcomed, respected, valued, and represented. Younger students can create or find images that illustrate these concepts. They can identify these concepts in picture books or social scripts.

Literature can be used with older students. Students in upper elementary and older can also create scenarios where they have had positive experiences and where negative experiences with these concepts could be encountered.

Have students reflect on questions such as the following:
1. How does inclusivity differ from just being present in a space? Can you think of an example where you truly felt included versus just being there?
2. What actions can you take to make someone truly feel more included in your group or team?

Students should learn the difference between intent and impact and that there are times when policies or plans are put in place with the best intent but may not bring about the intended impact. They will learn that assessment is a way to determine impact and can affect how change can happen. Methods for assessing a sense of belonging can be as simple as asking students informally or creating formal surveys that student, parents, and even faculty and staff can complete. The Student Belonging Channel covered in this section is another example of a method to assess a sense of belonging.

Older students can be involved in creating an assessment. They may think of questions for surveys and discuss the advantages and disadvantages to having an anonymous assessment.

Institutions often create or consult with organizations to create climate assessments that can measure and quantify a sense of inclusivity and belonging in a school community. Students can learn about best practices for soliciting, analyzing, and creating assessments of inclusivity and belonging.

Human Psychology

Empathy is understanding how another person feels without necessarily feeling what they feel or approving of it. Empathy is not sympathy, compassion, or pity; it is the act of using one's imagination to apprehend what another person is feeling.

There are activities students can participate in to expand their understanding of empathy.

1. Role-playing scenarios: Set up various scenarios where students can take on different roles and perspectives. For example, students could role-play a conflict between two classmates or a situation where someone is feeling excluded. Have students consider the emotions and perspectives of others. Create scenarios that involve situations where identity differences may lead to misunderstandings or conflicts (e.g., misgendering or touching someone hair without their permission). This should be done carefully as to not perpetuate stereotypes.
2. Storytelling and literature: Read stories or watch videos that depict characters experiencing different emotions and facing various challenges. Afterward, facilitate discussions about how the characters might be feeling and why. Encourage students to reflect on similar experiences they've had and how they would respond with empathy.
3. Empathy maps: Provide students with a template of an empathy map, which includes sections for thoughts, feelings, actions, and needs. Ask them to think about a specific person or group of people (e.g., a new student, someone experiencing a difficult situation), and fill in each section based on what they imagine the person might be thinking, feeling, doing, and needing. This helps students develop empathy by putting themselves in someone else's shoes.
4. Social Identity Prism: Have students use the Social Identity Prism to think about the different parts of their identity. Then, facilitate a discussion about how these different identities can influence people's behaviors, perspectives, and experiences. Encourage students

to reflect on their own identities and consider how they shape their interactions with others.

Socialization is the processes, explicit or implicit, by which individuals acquire worldviews, beliefs, values, and codes of conduct that align with and reflect the norms of the groups in which they are socialized.

The concept may be harder for elementary-aged students to fully grasp. However, older students can be introduced to the Cycle of Socialization. The concept of socialization and the Cycle of Socialization can be adapted and can be developmentally appropriate for middle school– and high school–aged students. This can be aligned with Health & Wellness curricula and dovetails with conversations about peer pressure and agency.

Other activities could include the following:
1. Family Socialization Timeline: Older students could create a timeline of significant events or experiences in their lives that have influenced their views, values, and beliefs. Encourage them to consider how their family background and beliefs and cultural heritage have shaped their perspectives on social identity, bias, and justice issues. Facilitate a discussion where students can share and reflect on the similarities and differences in their experiences.
2. Analyzing Media: Starting in middle school, students can use a selection of media resources, such as news articles, advertisements, shows, or social media posts that portray various social identities, biases, and justice issues. Guide students through a critical analysis of how these media representations influence perceptions and reinforce or dispel stereotypes and biases. Have children reflect on their own media consumption habits and how they contribute to their understanding of social issues.

Private belief refers to an individual's personal convictions, values, and beliefs that are held privately and may not be openly expressed or shared with others. These beliefs can include religious, moral, political, or cultural perspectives that shape an individual's identity and worldview. On the other hand, public tolerance refers to society's acceptance and respect for diverse beliefs, opinions, and practices, even when they differ from one's own.

The tension between private belief and public tolerance arises when individuals or groups hold beliefs that conflict with societal norms, laws, or the rights and freedoms of others. This tension raises questions about the extent to which individuals should be allowed to express their private beliefs in public spaces, especially when those beliefs may cause harm or offense to others.

There are times when what is taught in an educational setting does not match with the private beliefs of a family. Any diverse setting will have members who have multiple perspectives on various issues. Even when parents have the ability to choose an independent or parochial school for their child, there may be times when a family's values, worldviews, and codes of conduct do not align with that of the school's. Students will learn how to reconcile what their family may believe or what they may believe and how they behave, react, and function at school and/or in other public spaces.

For instance, a child may be taught certain religious beliefs about LGBTQ+ identities from their family. At school, they may be taught that all different types of families are equally important and respected.

Students will learn that they can hold on to their private beliefs and also exist in a public space that can hold many different beliefs, even those that are contrary to the ones they have at home. Students will understand the importance of being able to hold a private belief and still tolerate other beliefs in public.

Technically, a prejudice is simply a disposition towards something or a person or group that is not necessarily based on actual experience with the thing or people (to pre-judge). In common usage, the term typically connotes unfair negative constructions of people or groups.

"Stereotype" comes from the term for creating templates for printing that can be used over and over without variation. This idea, when applied to understanding human beings, refers to casting people with unique qualities into a sameness that can be reductive and even offensive.

Racialization is the process by which a single human mind, a community of human minds, or an entire society creates the concept and construct of race and the associated ideology, doctrine, and practice of racism. It involves the five steps:
1. Selecting some human characteristics as meaningful signs of human difference
2. Sorting people int subpopulations based on selected distinctions
3. Attributing traits to the subpopulations
4. Essentializing the differences – conceiving them as natural, immutable, and hereditary
5. Acting as if the differences justify unequal treatment

The Social Identity Prism and the Cauldron of Social Bias can be used to reach this learning outcome. Every ism is a version of the human tendency to reduce complicated and whole beings to members of narrow essentialized social identity groups, to rank the constructed groups as better or worse in various ways, and to favor or disfavor perceived members accordingly.

Grasping the importance and the dynamics of social bias concepts deepens over the years as students learn how each ism was used for power and control throughout world history and throughout the histories of content areas such as math, science, art, etc.

It is important for students to understand that although these topics can generate strong emotions and feelings, there is a way to discuss and learn about these concepts as scholars, not representative, victims, or villains. Understanding there is a way to learn, evaluate, synthesize and critique the application of these concepts with a critical thinking lens maintains a level of scholarship that can be lost in arguments grounded in opinions and personal preferences.

Using protocols that outline how critical thinking can be applied to all scholarly discussions can create consistency and neutrality to debates and readings. Systems for grounding learning in research, using sources that are reputable, providing multiple perspectives all create spaces where complex, respectful, and factual discussions can expand the learning of all individuals.

Key human psychology concepts can be closely tied to social studies and history curricula. Examples from the past or present can be used in case studies and media analysis and role-playing or discussions on ethics.

DEI Choices

The DEI Choices DWD Antibias Standards engage students in the crucial exercise of personal synthesis. Rather than presenting students with a set of prescriptions for what their learnings through the Identity, Diversity, Equity, Inclusivity, and Human Psychology standards should be in terms of attitude and behavior, the final standard upholds the responsibility to respect students' agency and right to determine their own bearing on what they learn.

The synthesis activity will take the form of creating a "Personal Wishes" and a "Commitment Letter."

DEI Choices – How I Wish to Be Treated

Each student will create a "Personal Wishes Statement" in which they describe how they hope to be treated by others considering their complex social identities. The charter will be formatted as follows:

"I have learned that although every person is a complex combination of identities, our human brains sometimes lead us to think about and treat people as if they were just one identity. I have learned that sometimes we can have positive or negative ideas about an identity we think someone has. Here's how I hope people treat me when they think about me in terms of the Social Identity Prism categories."

Family-Ethnicity-Heritage – I hope . . .
Physical Appearance – I hope . . .
Age – I hope . . .
Ability – I hope . . .
Gender – I hope . . .
Sexual Orientation – I hope . . .
Racialization – I hope . . .
Social Status – I hope . . .
Worldview-Ideology – I hope . . .
+ Something else about me – I hope . . .

Students will be invited to share these reflections in a supportive classroom environment, fostering understanding and empathy. This would be optional.

DEI Choices Commitment Letter

Students will articulate their individual goals for treating others in terms of diversity, equity, and inclusivity, using what they have learned through the Social Identity Prism.

Each student will draft "Commitment Letters" where they make pledges on how they will treat others, recognizing the full spectrum of social identities. The letter will be formatted as follows.

"I understand that every person is a complex combination of identities and that it's easy for us to simplify someone down to a single identity. Here's how I commit to treating others when I interact with them, considering the Social Identity Prism categories, ensuring that I resist the tendency to reduce people to restrictive categories and engage with them based on a holistic view of their personhood."

Family-Ethnicity-Heritage – I will . . .
Physical Appearance – I will . . .
Age – I will . . .
Ability – I will . . .
Gender – I will . . .
Sexual Orientation – I will . . .
Racialization – I will . . .
Social Status – I will . . .
Worldview-Ideology – I will . . .
+ Something else about me – I will . . .

Examples of DEI Choices statements: The following four imagined statements are not meant to be prescriptive in any way. Instead, they are meant to provide students with some sense of what a student from the indicated background might express. Every student should feel encouraged to express their authentic views in their statement, and there will be no judgment about what students write (barring hateful or threatening language, of course).

The imagined expressions cleave towards tolerance but do so in a way that respects the likelihood that some students will hold private beliefs that do not represent DEI-expansivist goals. Because most schools are bound and committed to expansivist antibias principles and practices, it seems most useful to provide models that reflect ways that all students can maintain their personal views (including restrictivist views) and also demonstrate public tolerance.

The examples that follow are geared to be of use for older elementary-age students and onward through high school. As with all curricula, teachers are the vital and necessary moderators and adapters of material to ensure that students engage with developmentally appropriate content.

For younger learners, a category-by-category approach should perhaps be replaced by a general consideration of how the students want to be treated in terms of fairness and how they will treat others fairly no matter any differences between them. This approach might be facilitated by using picture books that focus on fair treatment and examples of "real life" examples from the school day (e.g., being allowed into a game at recess or allowing a new person to sit at the lunch table or learning to pronounce someone's name as they wish it to be pronounced).

Example 1: How I Wish to be Treated Statement – Student Facing Social Bias

> I have learned that although every person is a complex combination of identities, our human brains sometimes lead us to think about and treat people as if they were just one identity. Here's how I hope people treat me when they think about me in terms of the Social Identity Prism categories.
>
> Family-Ethnicity-Heritage – I hope to be respected for my cultural background, without people making negative assumptions and judgments about me because of where my family is from and our customs.
> Physical Appearance – I hope others will not feel they can always ask me where I'm from or "What am I?" or touch my hair because it's so different from theirs.
> Age – I hope people will see that I'm probably more mature than other kids my age because I've had to be.
> Ability – I hope people won't treat me like I'm dumb just because I didn't go to the same schools they did or have tutors. I hope I get the chance to learn and show I can be as smart as anyone.

Gender – I hope people will respect my right to define my own identity and call me by the name I use, not the name they think I should use.

Sexual Orientation – I hope people will let me love who I love even if it doesn't match their idea of who should be allowed to love who.

Racialization – I hope people will treat me equally even though I have darker skin than they do.

Social Status – I hope not having a lot of money won't lead people to think my parents don't work very hard.

Worldview-Ideology – I hope my family's religious beliefs and practices won't be treated like they're weird or wrong.

Something else about me – I hope that my quiet nature isn't taken the wrong way. I'm quiet because I'm shy and I'm still learning about this country, not because I'm stuck up.

Example 2: Commitment Letter – Student with Unearned Social Advantages

I understand that every person is a complex combination of identities and that it's easy for us to simplify someone down to a single identity. Here's how I commit to treating others when I interact with them, considering the Social Identity Prism categories, ensuring that I resist the tendency to reduce people to restrictive categories and engage with them based on a holistic view of their personhood.

Family-Ethnicity-Heritage – I will treat everyone with respect no matter where they come from. Honestly, I've been treated badly by people who seem to think that just because they are true Americans or whatever, they're better than me – and I hate that, but I know I should remember that everyone who shares any background isn't necessarily going to act the same way. I know people who have deep roots in America and Europe who are fair and nice too.

Physical Appearance – I will always treat people based on what they stand for and what they do, not on how they look. Looks are an accident for the most part. What you do is about the choices you make.

Ability – I will always try to find what someone is good at or wants to be good at and admire them for their effort even if it doesn't always result in greatness.

Gender – I will respect everyone's gender identity. I don't even understand why it matters. We should just let people be who they are as long as they are letting people be who they are.

Sexual Orientation – Same as earlier. Love is love.

Racialization – I will stop thinking and talking about people like they are members of a category that doesn't even exist. We're humans; all of us; end of story.

Social Status – I will not hold my friends responsible for what their parents have or don't have – money, resources, power. We're just kids. We shouldn't flaunt it if we have wealthy families, and we shouldn't look down on kids who don't come from money and power.

Worldview-Ideology – I will respect everyone's right to have whatever views they have as long as they do the same for me. We don't have to agree on everything; just on the importance of being tolerant.

Something Else about Me – I will help this world move beyond crazy and deadly conflicts based on bad assumptions and oppressive beliefs. We've got to do better than we've been doing.

Example 3: Commitment Letter – Student with Unearned Social Advantages

I understand that every person is a complex combination of identities and that it's easy for us to simplify someone down to a single identity. Here's how I commit to treating others when I interact with them, considering the Social Identity Prism categories, ensuring that I resist the tendency to reduce people to restrictive categories and engage with them based on a holistic view of their personhood.

Family-Ethnicity-Heritage – I will treat everyone with respect no matter where they come from. Just because everyone's family hasn't been in this country for generations doesn't mean everyone shouldn't feel as American as any other American.

Physical Appearance – I will remember that I wouldn't like it if people asked me all the time where I'm from or "What are you?", and I won't ask others those questions. If I want to know more about someone, I'll ask them if they'd mind telling me about themselves, and see what they say – and I'll share about myself too.

Ability – I will understand that it's OK to have different learning styles and goals and talents and not judge anyone by the grades they get or how good an athlete they are.

Gender – I will try to remember what we learned about private beliefs and public tolerance – and even though I was taught that there are only two genders and homosexuality is not right, I won't make people who don't believe that feel bad or wrong.

Sexual Orientation – Answered earlier.

Racialization – I will use my advantages to challenge racial injustices and support anti-racist actions.

Social Status – I will not make people feel bad about being from a family that might not have as many resources as mine. I'll watch how I talk about money and the stuff I get to buy and the trips my family gets to take.

Worldview-Ideology – I will respect everyone's right to have whatever faith they have or even to not believe in anything spiritual at all. I know I'm lucky that my religion is pretty dominant in society, and that that can be hard for people whose beliefs don't match mine.

Something Else about Me – I will try to use my privileges to help people who face bias feel supported.

Example 4: How I Wish to Be Treated Statement – Student with Restrictivist Views

I have learned that although every person is a complex combination of identities, our brains sometimes lead us to think about and treat people as if they were just one identity. Despite my personal beliefs about certain identities, here's how I hope people will treat me when they think about me in terms of the Social Identity Prism categories.

Family-Ethnicity-Heritage – I hope the fact that my family and relatives benefited and still benefit from unearned privilege doesn't lead people to treat me like I created social inequality and want to keep things unequal. I don't.

Physical Appearance – I hope that if people think I'm good-looking or attractive or whatever, they don't act like that's the most important thing about me – more important than what I think and what I do. I won't lie and say it's not nice to be liked, but I want to be liked and loved for who I am, not how I look.

Age – I hope that people won't try to take advantage of me because I may look older than I am but I only know what I know at my age.

Ability – I hope people won't blame me or not like me because some things come easily to me. I try to work as hard as I can to do my best even in things that do come easily to me.

Gender – I hope that my belief in there being just two genders will be tolerated just like I tolerate that some people believe there can be a whole range of ways to identify by gender.

> Sexual Orientation – I hope I won't be seen as the enemy because I'm a heterosexual person who's uncomfortable with the idea of homosexuality but wouldn't ever try to make anybody who's homosexual feel bad for being who they are.
> Racialization – I hope I won't be racialized as inherently, essentially racist because of how I look.
> Social Status – I hope my luck in being born to a family that has wealth and resources won't lead people to see me as someone who looks down on people who don't have a lot of money or power.
> Worldview-Ideology – I hope people will be as tolerant of my religious, political, and other beliefs as I try to be of theirs.
> Something Else about Me – I know I said it already, but I really hope people don't treat me like I'm the problem or the enemy just because of how I look and how I'm racialized. I feel like I can't win a lot of the time because I want to be on the right side of things, be a good ally, and work for inclusivity, but I feel like some people treat me like I don't have the right to even try to help.

Conclusion

The Diversity Without Divisiveness Antibias Standards provide students with knowledge and skills and allows them the freedom to form their own conclusions and actions. It prioritizes critical thinking and personal development so that students are empowered to apply their learning in ways that are meaningful to them.

As with all content areas, formative and summative assessments should be utilized to gauge if learning outcomes have been met and how differentiation, whether challenge or support, are necessary to help students meet outcomes. Concepts and skills should spiral throughout early, elementary, middle, and upper school years in order for students to apply knowledge in more complex and developmentally appropriate content areas.

Learning outcomes are based on students' understanding of facts and acquiring skills. After learning information, students have the agency to determine their own course of action, perspectives, and attitudes towards it. They may choose different paths or responses based on their understanding and beliefs. Students are encouraged to engage with information critically, fostering intellectual independence and analytical skills.

Diversity Without Divisiveness Anchor Standards

Learning for Justice Social Justice Standards (from learningforjustice.org)	Diversity Without Divisiveness Antibias Anchor Standards
Identity 1. Students will develop positive identities based on their membership in multiple groups in society. 2. Students will develop language and historical and cultural knowledge that affirm and accurately describe their membership in multiple identity groups. 3. Students will recognize that people's multiple identities interact and create unique and complex individuals. 4. Students will express pride, confidence, and healthy self-esteem without denying the value and dignity of other people. 5. Students will recognize traits of the dominant culture, their home culture, and other cultures and understand how they negotiate their own identity in multiple spaces.	Identity 1. Students will understand the meaning of the concept of identity. 2. Students will understand the difference between personal and social identity. 3. Students will understand the interaction between personal and social identity. 4. Students will recognize that people's multiple identities interact to create unique and complex individuals. 5. Students will understand that identity often serves as the basis of pride, belonging, and solidarity with others who share one's identity. 6. Students will understand that identity often serves as the basis for excluding those who do not share one's identity. 7. Students will understand the differences between scientific, empirical methods of categorizing human differences and unscientific social customs of group categorization. 8. Students will understand the primary social identity categories.
Diversity 1. Students will express comfort with people who are both similar to and different from them and engage respectfully with all people.	Diversity 1. Students will understand that diversity is inherent and essential to all forms of life, including human beings.

(Continued)

(Continued)

Learning for Justice Social Justice Standards (from learningforjustice.org)	Diversity Without Divisiveness Antibias Anchor Standards
2. Students will develop language and knowledge to accurately and respectfully describe how people (including themselves) are both similar to and different from each other and others in their identity groups. 3. Students will respectfully express curiosity about the history and lived experiences of others and will exchange ideas and beliefs in an open-minded way. 4. Students will respond to diversity by building empathy, respect, understanding, and connection. 5. Students will examine diversity in social, cultural, political, and historical contexts rather than in ways that are superficial or oversimplified.	2. Students will understand that there are macro-commonalities, mezzo-commonalities, and micro qualities across and within the human species. 3. Students will understand the benefits of diversity when effective equity and inclusivity are in place, and how diversity can result in conflict when effective equity and inclusivity measures are not in place.
Justice 1. Students will recognize stereotypes and relate to people as individuals rather than representatives of groups. 2. Students will recognize unfairness on the individual level (e.g., biased speech) and injustice at the institutional or systemic level (e.g., discrimination). 3. Students will analyze the harmful impact of bias and injustice on the world, historically and today.	Equity 1. Students will understand that equity means everyone getting what they need to have equal opportunities, not everyone getting the same thing or achieving the same outcomes. 2. Students will understand inequitable treatment associated with each primary social identity group. 3. Students will understand how social bias operates.

Learning for Justice Social Justice Standards (from learningforjustice.org)	Diversity Without Divisiveness Antibias Anchor Standards
4. Students will recognize that power and privilege influence relationships on interpersonal, inter-group, and institutional levels and consider how they have been affected by those dynamics. 5. Students will identify figures, groups, events, and a variety of strategies and philosophies relevant to the history of social justice around the world.	4. Students will understand how laws, policies, and practices are designed to create equity and social justice.
Action 1. Students will express empathy when people are excluded or mistreated because of their identities and concern when they themselves experience bias. 2. Students will recognize their own responsibility to stand up to exclusion, prejudice, and injustice. 3. Students will speak up with courage and respect when they or someone else has been hurt or wronged by bias. 4. Students will make principled decisions about when and how to take a stand against bias and injustice in their everyday lives and will do so despite negative peer or group pressure. 5. Students will plan and carry out collective action against bias and injustice in the world and will evaluate what strategies are most effective.	Inclusion 1. Students will understand that inclusivity means everyone being welcome, respected, valued, and represented in their communities, resulting in a sense of belonging and inclusion. 2. Students will understand methods for assessing a sense of inclusion/belonging.

(*Continued*)

(Continued)

Learning for Justice Social Justice Standards (from learningforjustice.org)	Diversity Without Divisiveness Antibias Anchor Standards
–	<u>Human Psychology</u> 1. Students will understand the concept and application of empathy as crucial in understanding behavioral differences associated with identity. 2. Students will understand how socialization shapes a person's views, values, and choices regarding social identity, social bias, and social justice issues. 3. Students will understand the important differences and tension between private belief and public tolerance. 4. Students will understand the social bias concepts of prejudice, stereotyping, racialization, and the specific forms of bias ("isms") associated with each primary social identity category. 5. Students will understand how to apply critical thinking to challenging situations and dynamics associated with diversity, equity, and inclusion and social identity, social bias, and social justice.

Touchstone/Tool #11: Creating a K–12 School Policy for Responding to Non-Curricular Societal Issues

This tool equips educators with principles, policy, and practices regarding the challenging issue of how best to respond to inevitable occurrences of issues in greater society that interest, involve, or impact members of the school community so strongly that they might warrant deliberate ad hoc integration one way or another into the educational program.

This section is presented in the form of a letter to the parents of Our School that informs them about Our School's Policy for Responding to Non-curricular Societal Issues.

Dear Our School Parents

This policy outlines Our School's commitment to addressing high-profile societal issues that warrant ad hoc integration into the education program within a framework that maintains educational neutrality and upholds our mission to provide accurate and developmentally appropriate information and safe space for all students to synthesis their own bearing on any given issue.

This policy will be clearly stated in student, staff, and parents' handbooks, reviewed at the start of each year, and again at the start of each term, along with an update of any high-profile societal issues discussion that have occurred since the last policy review.

The Policy Covers the Following Areas
1. Guiding principles
2. Non-partisanship
3. Neutral, civil, constructive engagement with issues and each other
4. Determining when high-profile issues should be integrated into the educational program
5. Politically partisan issues, symbols/displays, and freedom of expression
6. Key implementation considerations
7. Five circumstances to illustrate and explicate policy application
8. Societal Issues Response Protocol

1. Guiding Principle: Institutional Mission and Values: Our primary commitment is to educate. At Our School that means we provide factual information and facilitate learners' capacity to think critically, exchange perspective civilly and constructively, and synthesize their

own bearing on everything they encounter. We engage with societal issues through this mission-driven educational lens, focusing on fostering critical scrutiny and understanding without advocating for partisan positions and without endorsing or adopting stances of external sources with the exception of those coincide so closely with our own mission, values, commitments, and aspirations that they are practically interchangeable. As with everything we do at Our School, we seek to capitalize on the power diversity when mediated by effective equity and inclusivity measures to optimize learning about and discussing emergent high-profile societal issues.

2. Non-Partisanship: We are dedicated to preserving the non-partisan nature of our educational environment. Our role is to facilitate the exploration of ideas in a manner that supports learning and personal growth. Our role is not to seduce, persuade, or coerce students into attitudinal or behavioral positions. Our responsibility and joy are to foster critical thinking skills, constructive communication skills, self-awareness, and empathy, provide factual information, create an environment where students can feel safe enough to be brave enough to engage with challenging topics and each other, and to trust them to synthesize their own bearing on everything they encounter.

3. High-Profile Events: The school will address high-profile events that significantly impact our students or our educational process. School leaders will determine which issues warrant ad hoc integration into the educational program through thoughtful consideration of a range of factors including the levels of interest, involvement, and impact associate with any given issues. These events will be discussed in a manner consistent with our educational objectives and without endorsing specific political actions or movements.

4. Safe Exploration of Ideas: The school will ensure that discussions around high-profile issues provide a safe space for all students to explore and exchange diverse perspectives. These discussions will be facilitated toward staying focused on learning understanding.

Key Consideration Regarding Implementation

Information and Resources: The school will provide students with access to accurate, vetted information about societal issues. This may include bringing in non-partisan subject-matter experts, providing curated reading lists, or facilitating access to primary source materials.

Professional Development: Teachers and staff will receive training on how to discuss societal issues in a neutral, informative manner, and how to facilitate student discussions that are inclusive and reflective. This aspect of the policy is explicated in the Societal Issues Response Protocol section later.

Parental Communication: The school will communicate its policy and approach to parents, emphasizing our commitment to neutrality and the educational mission.

Monitoring and Evaluation: The school will regularly monitor and evaluate the effectiveness of the policy, seeking feedback from students, parents, and educators to ensure that the approach remains consistent with our guiding principles.

Five circumstances to illustrate and explicate policy application
1. School-sponsored social justice symbols and displays
2. Students or teachers wearing social justice symbols or displaying them on their items (laptops, water bottles, etc.)
3. Safe space symbols
4. Politically partisan symbols and displays
5. Global conflicts

1. School-sponsored social justice symbols and displays
Policy Application: Our School's statement on external sources of social justice messaging

At Our School Whoever You Are, However You Are, You Are Safe Here

At Our School, the expansive tapestry of diversity weaves through every classroom, every event, every program and event, every hallway, and every heart, creating a vibrant community bound by mutual respect and understanding. We stand firm in our dedication to creating an environment where every individual is valued, our commonalities are cherished, and our differences are understood as part and parcel of being human. In this spirit, Our School does not display external symbols or adopt external messaging to express our foundational commitments to anti-discrimination, antibias, and inclusivity.

Our decision stems from a deep-seated belief that the most profound declarations are not those borrowed from outside entities, whose broader agendas and interpretations we cannot control, but those that originate from within our own walls – crafted, supported, and lived by our community, posted on our walls, hanging from our rafters, extolled at our assemblies, and emblazoned on our apparel. While external movements and messages may align with our values in small or great part, they can carry a myriad of implications and associations that extend beyond our school's mission and dedication to non-partisanship. We choose not to risk the potential confusion or division that such affiliations might sow within our diverse community.

We take this stance not out of a lack of solidarity with any given externally advocated cause but out of a profound responsibility to uphold a space where each student, staff member, and family can engage with complex societal issues from a place of education, reflection, and personal growth. Ours is a space free from the presumption of consensus on external ideologies or political movements. Our goal is to provide students with factual information, critical thinking and communication skills, and a safe space in which to be brave enough to explore and exchange views on complicated and controversial issues.

Therefore, we assert our school's commitment through our own carefully considered expression and actions. Our policies, our curriculum, our professional development, and our community initiatives are all reflective of this unwavering commitment: to build a school where discrimination finds no foothold, bias is resisted and repelled, and inclusivity is as natural and common as the laugher and camaraderie that characterizes our interactions.

At Our School, you are safe to be who you are, to express your thoughts, to question, to challenge, and to grow. Our statement – Whoever You Are, However You Are, You Are Safe Here – is a promise, a practice, and a commitment to every member of our community, championed not merely by the symbols we display but by the daily actions we take and the culture of inclusivity we foster together.

2. Students or teachers wearing social justice symbols or displaying them on their items (laptops, water bottles, etc.)

Policy Application: Displays on personal apparel and goods is generally considered a form of personal expression, assuming it does not disrupt the educational environment or represent the endorsement of political views that might create a hostile environment for some community members.

3. Safe space symbols:

Policy Application: These symbols are often used to indicate a supportive and inclusive environment for all students, particularly marginalized groups, without reference to political views.

4. Politically partisan symbols and displays:

Policy Application: Our School refrains from posting symbols, images, messages, or displays that are politically partisan. Wearing political slogans could be considered personal expression and would likely be permissible as long as it does not disrupt educational activities. For teachers, it may be considered inappropriate if it impacts their neutrality in the classroom.

5. Global conflicts

Policy Application: The overall policy aims to create a learning environment where students are empowered to engage with complex global issues in ways that are informative, balanced, and non-partisan. By doing so, the policy helps to navigate the potential divisiveness such issues can bring into the school community. Here's how the policy would assist teachers, students, and parents in this context:

Information and Education: The policy would encourage teachers to provide students with factual, balanced information about the conflict. This could include the historical context, the perspectives of both Israelis and Palestinians, and the impact of the conflict on various communities. This approach would focus on education rather than taking sides.

Critical Thinking and Dialogue: Teachers would facilitate discussions that allow students to explore the conflict thoughtfully. This could involve debate, role-play, and research projects that help students understand the complexity of the issues without forcing a binary choice.

Safe and Inclusive Environment: The policy would guide schools to create a space where all students feel safe to express their views without fear of retribution or harassment.

Alignment with Educational Values: The policy would remind schools to refer to their institutional values when discussing the conflict. For instance, if a school values peace and conflict resolution, discussions could center on these themes, examining the conflict through the lens of how peace might be achieved.

Respecting Diversity of Opinion: Recognizing the diverse backgrounds and views within the school community, the policy would advise schools to ensure that no group feels marginalized or targeted because of their views on the conflict. This respect for diversity is essential for maintaining a positive learning environment.

Parental Engagement: The policy would involve parents by communicating the school's approach and encouraging them to contribute to a respectful, educational dialogue at home.

By applying such a policy, schools can encourage a nuanced, critical, and empathetic exploration of global issues, respecting the complexity of international conflicts and the variety of perspectives within the school community.

Societal Issues Response Protocol

At Our School, when a high-profile societal issue emerges, the following is done:
1. An administrator will alert all staff as to whether or not we will enact our Societal Issues Response Protocol.
2. Students and parents will be notified that in two or possibly three days, Our School will make factual information about the situation

and our Guide to Discussing High-profile Societal Issues Guide to support students and families that chose to discuss the topic outside of school to do so in ways that maximize civil and constructive conversation and reduce the risk of conflict.

3. Our Societal Issues Information and Resources Team will create and share a constellation of materials and resources for use in providing factual information to students and facilitation guidance to teachers who choose to use their course time to discuss the issue (because it is relevant to their course work and/or because the vast majority of their class group has expressed a strong desire to learn and explore the issues.
4. Students will be notified of opportunities to gather outside of their normally scheduled course work to voluntarily gather to learn crucial factual information about the issue and exchange questions, feeling, and views in a civil and constructive manner with adult facilitation.
5. Parents will receive summaries of discussions.
6. Students, staff, or family members who are directly and disproportionately impacted by the issues will be cared for in every reasonable way within the parameters of compassion, professional boundaries, and school resources (e.g., opportunities to gather to share feelings, information, and mutual support, referral to sources of support, etc.)

By implementing this policy, Our School aims to provide a structured, thoughtful approach to engaging with high-profile societal issues in a way that supports educational goals, respects diverse viewpoints, and nurtures students' ability to form their own informed opinions.

Notes

1 North Atlantic Treaty Organization. (2024, March 11). *10 Things You Need to Know about NATO*. Retrieved from https://www.nato.int/cps/en/natohq/126169.htm
2 Allport, G. W. (1955). *Becoming: Basic Considerations for a Psychology of Personality*. Yale University Press.
3 Rogers, C. R. (1995). *A Way of Being*. Houghton Mifflin.
4 Rorty, R. (2009). *Contingency, Irony, and Solidarity*. Cambridge University Press.

5 Morning, A. (2011). *The Nature of Race: How Scientists Think and Teach about Human Difference*. University of California Press.
6 Hoyt, C. (2021, June 12). Charting a course beyond racism [Video]. *TEDx Talks*. Retrieved from https://www.ted.com/talks/carlos_hoyt_charting_a_course_beyond_racism?language=en
7 Riegel, D. G. (2023, April 6). Your students aren't giving you useful feedback – Here's why: Overcome these 5 barriers to get the input you need. *Harvard Business Publishing*. Retrieved from https://hbsp.harvard.edu/inspiring-minds/your-students-arent-giving-you-useful-feedback-heres-why

PART THREE

Praxis Pointers

Real-World Applications from Educators in the Field

Praxis Pointer Contributor: Ian Arawjo

Contact Information: ianarawjo.com
The DEI Touchstone/Tool featured in my Praxis Pointer: Understanding Racialization

Some information about Ian

I am currently Assistant Professor of HCI at Université de Montréal. Previously I was a PhD student at Cornell, which is where I first encountered Dr. Hoyt's work. My dissertation focus was on "programming and culture," and one of the aspects was the "programming in culture," which is related to Dr. Hoyt's work. This research was in computer science (CS) education at the K–12 level.

The Educational Context in Which I Applied the Touchstone/Tool

Workshop with students (sixth grade), and educators in computer science education

My Motivation to Use the Touchstone/Tool

Following work in Kenya on how cross-ethnic groups collaborate in an intro computer programming class setting, I became interested in connections between concepts in programming and concepts in sociology, specifically social categories are created and maintained as kind of "algorithms" – what we later called "cultural algorithms" – embedded in cultures/societies.

Coming home to the U.S., I wondered how to create a "cultural algorithms" activity that touched on the salient "social groups" that are present (or apparently present) in the U.S. How can we get people to reflect on the arbitrariness of social categorization? At the same time, I was also reading *Racecraft* by Barbara and Karen Fields.[1]

Race is particularly important here because race in the U.S. is assumed to be "fixed," but those who walk the "line" like Adrian Piper (who can "pass" for white) see how arbitrary it is. The thesis of the Fields that racism creates race challenged me, and after reading the book many times, I started to internalize the concept. Later I read more widely, and two works stick in my mind: Carlos Hoyt's work and Rainier Spencer's work. The final suggestions of both Hoyt and Spencer are remarkably similar. However, Spencer grew disillusioned – on a podcast he suggested we already know how to solve the racialization problem; the trouble is that people in the U.S. do not want to change; they cling to their social categories like a security blanket.

Later, I read Adrian Piper's book *Escape to Berlin*[2] and learned this is largely why she left the U.S. – she grew frustrated that no one seemed to be really listening to what her work was really saying.

Details of How I Applied the Touchstone/Tool

I found Dr. Hoyt's steps of racialization in a Google Slides link on his site (I believe). It immediately stood out to me as an algorithm, and we began thinking how we could create an activity about it (I was working with Ariam Mogos, who is now a lecturer at Stanford). At the time racial matters were particularly heated, and so we were wondering how we could approach the racialization framework indirectly, letting students make the connections themselves rather than speaking directly about them (at least at first).

I believe Dr. Hoyt also does this in one of his activities. We created the activity "Birdcraft" which is described in my dissertation "Programming and Culture." Birdcraft, a play on racecraft, includes a worksheet of the steps of racialization but applies them to a fictional bird world, where height is the major discriminator of social groups. Groups are tasked to rethink bird world's racialization steps to make them more "fair" for everyone.

The activity was deliberately open-ended and is kind of a trick question – we wanted students to engage in the concepts and come to their own conclusion that racialization itself should be done away with. However, the cultural algorithms of Bird World (also referred to as "Birdcraft") allowed us to indirectly discuss concepts like reparations, passing, inconsistencies, who should decide (i.e., should the bird group with all the power have a voice in decisions?), and conflicts between self-identifying as a member a category and the potential collective social good to do away with the categorization.

The Impact of the Application of This Touchstone/Tool and How I Determined the Impact

This activity really had an impact on people, especially the educators we talked to. The conversations got deeper the longer the session lasted. Some of it is described in my dissertation. I wish (this was during COVID, so everything was virtual) we had run more sessions with students and educators, because this activity had great potential and would've made a highly interesting publication. I am happy to make the resources available, too.

Tips to Keep in Mind if You're Thinking about Using This Touchstone/Tool

Zvi Bekerman[3] talks about how children are not as attached to social categories as adults, because they are not yet encultured into the existing regime, and that we need to "sustain children's categories" if we are to improve intractable group conflicts. So, children could probably just do Birdcraft, or even an activity on Racecraft, directly; they are not going to be hesitant. It is the adults, especially the educators we talked to, who appeared extremely wary (including educators who identify as Black) about talking about racialization directly (not racism, but race). They perceived that talking about race from a social category standpoint trivializes racism, and I believe this perception comes from their strong belief that race produces racism, rather than the opposite (race is naturalized to them).

So, as in any culture, when someone challenges one's core culture precepts, that organize their society, they are liable to react with hostility. It was also the case that for myself, as someone who is identified as white in the U.S., they were more hostile to the idea than they would've been otherwise. So, it was a strategy of ours to make Birdcraft use the racialization steps to talk about racialization indirectly, at first, as a springboard to get people thinking critically before holding those deeper conversations. That is, we could sidestep "telling people what to think" and let them come to their own conclusions first.

For more information on Birdcraft, please see "CS for Racial Literacy: Teaching Race through Cultural Algorithms: Can computing concepts help kids learn about race?" Medium. February 15, 2021. https://aninjustice-mag.com/cs-for-racial-literacy-teaching-race-through-cultural-algorithms-8a1be4666c7b.

Special Notes about Contacting Me for Consultation
I am really interested in educators who want to take the Birdcraft and apply it in their classes, including but not exclusive to computer/programming education. We didn't get to run the activity more than twice, which was a real shame.

Praxis Pointer Contributor: Jonathon Drummey

Contact Information: Please contact Jonathon at LinkedIn
The DEI Touchstone/Tool featured in my Praxis Pointer: The DEI
 Ally Pact

Some Information about Jonathon
Jonathan is a white-racialized educator who was born and raised in Boston, Massachusetts, and is currently living and working in California. With over ten years of experience as an educator and leader, Jonathan has worked in both public and private schools on both American coasts and enjoys the development, growth, and exploration that accompany children in early adolescence. An English teacher by training, Jonathan believes in the power of collaborative discussion and the serenity that a well-timed book can bring to the mind. Jonathan graduated with a BA in English Literature from Saint Michael's College, an M.Ed in Secondary English Instruction from Boston College, and an Ed.M in Independent School Leadership from Columbia University. He believes deeply that children and adults are at their best when they experience belonging, and takes pride in leading people to accomplish their goals. He is currently serving as the Middle Division Director of Wildwood School in Los Angeles, California.

The Educational Context in Which I Applied the Touchstone/Tool
At an independent PreK to eighth-grade school outside of Boston with a total student population of 325 students.

My Motivation to Use the Touchstone/Tool
The DEI Ally Pact acknowledges that we all "have work to do." Part of this work is acknowledging harm when it occurs and taking the next steps to educate oneself to effectively learn and repair harm. Written in clear language, the guidelines embedded in the Ally Pact are approachable for students and adults. Additionally, the Ally Pact lays out something critical for institutions committed to learning – it creates space for mistakes and encourages dialogue and growth. It is a community code that all folks can get on board with and promotes healthy dialogue across a spectrum of identities and between ages and status levels within an educational context.

Details of How I Applied the Touchstone/Tool
"I'm sure you heard about the incident involving the girls." The declaration caught me off guard. As two parents discussed the racialized microaggression

their bi-racial daughter and Latinx peer experienced from a senior administrator, I was left stunned and frustrated. Shifting our parent conference conversation from a celebration of this student's academic acumen and good standing in our community, I listened as they relayed their daughter's pain before boarding the bus home. Accused of stealing food labeled "free snacks" and being called a liar for defending her actions, this student was in psychological distress and questioned her level of belonging in our school community. Staring back into the two-by-three zoom box of our conference and hearing the hurt they felt inside as their daughter processed this was devastating. Thankfully, our school had laid some groundwork around belonging and specifically had a protocol for addressing microaggressions. I assured the family that such an incident was wrong and that our school had a structure to repair this appropriately – the DEI Ally Pact.

The Impact of the Application of This Touchstone/Tool and How I Determined the Impact

Following my parent conference, I immediately reached out to the offending administrator. I cited our community, "Ally Pact," through email and stated my expectation that these children would receive an apology. I never heard back from this administrator. However, it was made clear that my efforts to directly call this senior leader to account for the harm they caused to children were not well received. The resistance that followed and the inability of this school leader to stand by and support our belonging initiatives led to the ultimate resignation of our Director of Equity and Inclusion and the departure of three senior administrators at the end of the year.

After the children received an apology a week later, our Director of Equity and Inclusion resigned. In our Director of Equity and Inclusion's resignation, he wrote: "I left because I could not be a party to actions and inaction concerning the welfare and dignity of some of the most vulnerable members of society and the school community." The school's "inaction" following our Director of Equity and Inclusion's resignation was most concerning for some members of our faculty community. The school was not forthright about the reason behind our director's resignation, and the lack of honesty and transparency that followed was indicative of a culture where institutional resistance to enacting equity and inclusion work was acceptable.

While this moment broke my heart, it also revealed the school's inability to live its values and mission, and myself and numerous high-ranking administrators departed the school by the end of the year. The institution did not spare those it harmed its defensiveness. While the events following my initial conversation with the family did not transpire as I envisioned, they did receive a measure of closure for their children. In addition, I walked away with clarity on why the Ally Pact is an essential core practice for communities committed to equity and inclusion work. It is not simply a paper that we post in classrooms, but it is a practice of calling out hurt, inviting in reflection and expecting growth and reflection as the norm.

As an ally, choosing to leave because of microaggressions and lack of belonging should no longer be for our colleagues and families from traditionally marginalized backgrounds. It should be an action taken up in equal measure by our predominantly white teacher corps. School communities need to understand that what's at stake in equity and inclusion work is not just being fully enrolled but being institutionally capable of acceptably serving and extending belonging for all. When schools mess up, they should stand up. If those with the privileged identity markers our schools were designed and built to serve continue to accept incremental progress as policy, the system of being a home for some and not for all will continue. The Ally Pact is path forward towards justice and accountability.

Tips To Keep in Mind if You're Thinking about Using This Touchstone/Tool

Upheld as a standard for confronting a variety of bias that students, faculty, and staff may encounter, the Ally Pact is a code that works best if it is applied to an entire school community. Additionally, providing training on what the Ally Pact looks and feels like in action by providing a variety of different hypothetical scenarios will aid people when they will inevitably "have work to do."

Special Notes about Contacting Me for Consultation

Please reach out via LinkedIn if you would like to connect. I am experienced in middle division education and leadership.

Praxis Pointer Contributor: Cathy Giles

Contact Information: cgiles@crestcollborative.org
The DEI Touchstone/Tool featured in my Praxis Pointer: The Social Identity Prism

Some Information about Me
- Thirty-plus years of educational leadership and related experience
- Passionate about/targeted focus on trauma-informed practices, social-emotional teaching and learning, emotional intelligence, SEL/DEI/B-interconnectedness
- Holds Massachusetts Professional Certification in Special Education Administrator – all levels
- Superintendent/Asst. Superintendent – all levels, Special Education
- Certified National Board of Professional Teaching Standards
- Adjunct professor at local colleges
- Currently Director of SEL at a collaborative school in Massachusetts (Massachusetts Collaboratives are a statewide network of public educational service agencies that work together with school districts and schools to provide special education programs, both in-district and outplacement, particularly for students with multiple, complex learning, and therapeutic needs.)

The Educational Context in Which I Applied the Touchstone/Tool
Our overarching goal was that by using the Social Identify Prism through a collaborative art/non-threatening approach, students would make connections to their own lives and experiences and, as explained in the Prism tool, recognize the full spectrum of social identity and resist the tendency to reduce people to one or another restrictive category.

My Motivation to Use the Touchstone/Tool
I wanted to start the school year by cultivating a sense of belonging and connection for all students and staff across all programs through a collaborative art project. The Social Identity Prism was the perfect tool to use as our focus and really helped staff understand the interconnectedness of DEIB and SEL!

Details of How I Applied the Touchstone/Tool

Materials
- Colored copies of social identity prism
- Strips of colored paper (matching the colors in the prism)

- Tissue paper (matching the colors in the prism)
- Glue sticks (lots and lots and lots!)
- Tin foil

Introduce the Activity
We are going to use the Social Identity Prism to reflect upon and discuss different aspects of our own identities.

Present Essential Questions
1. How can your identity work as a lens through which you see the world?
2. What is your interpretation of the Social Identify Prism quote: "Whoever you are, however you are, you are safe here?"

Review
Prism, Identity Words, Definitions to Check for Understanding/Clarify Questions, etc.

Explain Steps
Students will use their paper copy of the prism and think about which aspects of themselves or identities are important to them identifying who they are right now.

Guiding Questions/Suggestions to Ask
1. What part of your identity do you think people first notice about you?
2. What part of your identity are you most comfortable sharing with other people?
3. What part of your identity are you least comfortable sharing with other people?
4. What part of your identity are you most proud of?

Personal Identity and Social Identity
Ask students to categorize those identities based on which matter most in their self-perception and which matter most in others' perception of them.

Students should be invited to place strips of paper with the Social Identity Prism social identity in the order that matches their self-perception and then how they feel others perceive them.

Reflection and Sharing
- Allow time for students to reflect on how they prioritized their identities.

- Invite students to share which identities they prioritized as most important to them, and if willing to do so, have them explain their reasoning.

Enrichment/Extension
- Students form pairs.
- Each student holds their top five identities of their prioritized list (or strips) in front of them so that the other student can't see them.
- Have each student pick one of the pieces of the strips from their partner's strips and read it aloud.

Ask All Students
1. How do you think you would feel if that identity was taken away from you?
2. What if you had to hide that identity from other people?
3. What if no one ever saw that part of your identity, that part of who you are?

Return to Essential Question
1. Encourage students to share their interpretation of the quote from the Prism: "Whoever you are, however you are, you are safe here."
2. Ask: What can we do to help others feel safe sharing all of who they are?

Additional Questions for Students to Consider
1. Ask students what would make them feel welcome to share more of their identities. Connect this to concerns about teasing/bullying, bystanders, etc. Acknowledge the difficulty some may have if/when they feel as if they need to hide parts of who they are or if they are teased or bullied for who they are.
2. Ask students if they have ideas on how everyone at school can create a community of learners where all know and feel safe and a sense of belonging.
3. Students can work on the collaborative art project at the same time as the group conversation so it feels more informal and also keeps students actively engaged!

The Impact of the Application of This Touchstone/Tool and How I Determined the Impact

Initially the Social Identity Prism and the quote "Whoever you are, however you are, you are safe here" was used for our school-wide sense of belonging "theme" for the month of September. Little did we realize how ONE colorful prism, ONE quote, and collaborative art project would help transform our culture and climate and the work that we do here for staff and students alike – its impact was significant and lasting!

Through our ongoing discussions across grade spans/age levels, our students and staff have become more socially and self-aware, and their ability to empathize, connect, and collaborate with a diverse group of peers is amazing to watch. It reminds us why we love what we do!

Tips to keep in mind if you're thinking about using this Touchstone/Tool (your advice to anyone who might want to apply this Touchstone/Tool)

Be mindful of how large you make the prism for the collaborative art project, because it requires a LOT of tissue paper pieces and glue sticks!

Special Notes about Contacting Me for Consultation
Please feel free to contact me at Cathy Giles Consultant at CG Consulting: https://www.linkedin.com/in/cathy-giles-53b96b203/

Praxis Pointer Contributors: Holly O'Leary and Robin LoConte, Capstone Teachers at New Liberty Innovation School (NLIS)

Some Information about Us
New Liberty Innovation School is a small high school located in Salem, Massachusetts. We are educators who are passionate about building relationships with our students; we reach before we teach. We work with students who have struggled in traditional high schools.

THE DEI TOUCHSTONE/TOOL FEATURED IN OUR PRAXIS POINTER: THE CYCLE OF SOCIALIZATION

The Educational Context in Which We Applied the Touchstone/Tool
Capstone class for seniors completing the Butterfly Effect Unit, which culminates in a storytelling piece shared both written and orally. With the addition of the cycle of socialization, students were asked to identify their personal disruption, "their butterfly effect" in their stories.

Our Motivation to Use the Touchstone/Tool
After experiencing our staff's reflections when learning about the Cycle of Socialization in a professional development workshop with Dr. Hoyt, we realized that including this in our Capstone task of personal change would deepen the work we are doing as a school.

Details of How We Applied the Touchstone/Tool
Please see our Capstone 2024 slides to get a good sense of how we used the Cycle of Socialization tool as well as other Diversity Without Divisiveness tools (Who Is This Person and the Social Identity Prism): https://docs.google.com/presentation/d/1U2prEnKDTadilUSR8qVE-eb_eCgTvyxUDmEl2azVT7k/edit#slide=id.g1f53e44eed0_2_6.

The Impact of the Application of This Touchstone/Tool and How We Determined the Impact
Students were able to gain deep insight into how their socialization was impacted beyond their own families and within larger systems as well. Students became aware of how they have the power to disrupt the negative impacts of the cycle of socialization. Examples: bullying, racialization, poverty, addiction, language barriers, etc.

Tips to Keep in Mind if You're Thinking about Using This Touchstone/Tool
As educators we have to be open and vulnerable about our own experiences so that we can honestly model the cycle to students. By sharing our own "disruptions" and reflection on the cycle, students see that they have the power to write their own story. Our power comes from our stories.

Please Feel Free to Contact the NLIS Team
Robin LoConte, Wellness Teacher/Counselor & Holly O'Leary, Academic Coach
    Teaching and Learning Team
    New Liberty Innovation School of Salem
    1 Museum Place Mall
    Suite 200
    Salem, MA 01970
    Main: (978)825–3470
    holeary@salemk12.org and rloconte@salemk12.org

Praxis Pointer Contributor: Lana Collier Holman

Some Information about Me
I began my teaching career in Tennessee in 1996. While I have taught most grades PreK through grade eight in both private and public schools, I have been teaching fourth graders at an independent private school in Massachusetts for the past 22 years. I teach reading, writing, and social studies, with a focus on storytelling and ancient civilizations.

THE DEI TOUCHSTONE/TOOL FEATURED IN MY PRAXIS POINTER: DEI ALLY PACT

The Educational Context in Which I Applied the Touchstone/Tool
I use the DEI Ally Pact as a tool to promote honest, direct communication with my students and their caregivers in the hopes that they feel seen, heard, and cared for in my classroom.

My Motivation to Use the Touchstone/Tool
My initial motivation to use the Ally Pact was Carlos. He introduced it to my school and encouraged us to share it with parents.

I will admit, initially I was quite nervous. The Ally Pact felt like it was asking so much of me. My co teacher saw beyond my fears and suggested we share the Ally Pact at our beginning-of-the-year Parent Listening Conferences, and that is what we did.

After one of those listening conferences, a family referred to it as they brought up a concern the first week of school. As we followed the guidelines laid out in the Pact, we had a challenging but productive conversation that set the tone for our relationship the remainder of the year. Every year since, when I share the Ally Pact, I think of that family, and it continues to be the parent and student relationships that motivate me to use the Ally Pact.

Details of How I Applied the Touchstone/Tool
There are three dimensions to how I apply the DEI Ally Pact in my classroom. First, I share it with my students and their caregivers at the beginning of the year. I speak to its importance, and I remind them of it (particularly the students) when difficult conversations are needed. For instance, after we finish a class meeting that addresses a complicated topic, I remind my students of the Ally Pact and tell them if they feel like they were not seen or heard, or if I said something that left them with a question or feeling uncomfortable, I

hope they are comfortable enough to let me or a trusted adult know. We then go over the established classroom methods for communicating with me.

Second, the Ally Pact informs how I communicate with parents. When a caregiver reaches out with a concern, I start by just listening, and I am always checking myself to make sure I am not going into a conversation on the defensive.

Lastly, I use it as a tool for self-reflection. If I walk away from a conversation feeling unsettled, I often think about the Ally Pact. I consider intent vs impact, I look for points where there may have been an opportunity for miscommunication (for example through language or cultural differences), I recognize if I am feeling or acting defensive and ask myself why, and I think about next steps.

The Impact of the Application of This Touchstone/Tool and How I Determined the Impact

When I am lucky, I receive feedback directly from a family, but in most cases the impact is found in self-reflection. I think about conversations and if families and students opened up and asked hard questions. Were families coming to me or my administrator? If I felt uncomfortable or defensive at any point, why did I feel that way, how did I respond, and what were the outcomes? What changes did I think about or make this year in response to a conversation? I feel that this reflection is key to making it a living document.

Tips to Keep in Mind if You're Thinking about Using This Touchstone/Tool

The DEI Ally Pact is not a program to be followed. It is a philosophical belief about how you would like to communicate, and, while there are small steps you can take (like sharing it at Back to School Night or putting it on the classroom wall), it will look and feel slightly different for everyone. Since it is not a program that needs to be adopted by a school system, it can be adopted and used in both public and private school settings. Take your time thinking about the words of the Pact and what they mean to you. Trust your gut (even when it is telling you what you don't want to hear), and let that guide you.

Once you introduce the Ally Pact, it does not need to be referred to daily. You will start to find ways to weave it into your daily practice. It can be as simple as the tone you set for class meeting or signing off an email about a conversation you had with a student by saying, "If you learn that your child did not feel seen or heard today, please reach out."

I think the DEI Ally Pact can seem overwhelming because, as teachers, we don't want to make mistakes that impact our students, but the reality is we are human and always learning and growing. The DEI Ally Pact is a reminder of our humanity and a tool to help us do the complicated work of being human together. In the end, it can actually make the work easier.

If you have any questions or want to brainstorm about how to implement the DEI Ally Pact, want to hear more examples of what it looks like in action, or just need some encouragement (like I did), please reach out via email: circeteaches@gmail.com.

Praxis Pointer Contributor: Heather Woodcock

Some Information about Me
I've worked in independent schools for the last 29 years as a classroom educator and as the assistant director and then director of a school-based teacher preparation program. Encouraging student teachers and their mentors to reflect upon and grow their practice with students has allowed me to continue to evolve and refine my own understanding of the hows, whats, and whys of the many moments and human interactions that take place in classrooms every day.

THE DEI TOUCHSTONE/TOOL FEATURED IN MY PRAXIS POINTER: THE SOCIAL IDENTITY PRISM

The Educational Context in Which I Applied the Touchstone/Tool
I have used the Social Identity Prism in my work with student teachers to build awareness of self, others, and curriculum development.

My Motivation to Use the Touchstone/Tool
I think teachers who seek to understand themselves and also embrace the many identities of their students and their families are better equipped to be successful and satisfied as educators. If the ultimate goal of the teacher is to help children learn, then the teacher must first ensure that their students feel safe, seen, heard, respected and free to ask questions and explore. So, in my work with student teachers, I have used the Social Identity Prism from the first day of our orientation together as a frame for building relationships and curriculum in the classroom.

Details of How I Applied the Touchstone/Tool
A poster of the social identity prism hangs in the student teacher seminar room all year long. On our first day together as a group, and after we have already established basic group norms, I introduce the image and give students time to examine it on their own and then choose two to three social identities to write about. In pairs, they are then given time to discuss any of the writing they chose to do. They do not need to share what they've written, and if they'd rather discuss the prism and their response to it in their pair, they are invited to do so.

After the pairs have had some time to talk, we engage in conversation as a group using the following prompts as a guide: What connections did you make during this exercise? What was challenging about this exercise? How does any of this apply to your work with students and colleagues in the classroom?

For our seminars over the following weeks, I ask each student teacher to bring an artifact (a picture, a book, a handout, a toy, or a short written reflection, etc.) that they see as representing the prism in their classroom or in the school as a whole.

Once student teachers have become more adept at writing lesson plans and units over the following months, they are asked to incorporate aspects of the social identity prism into their teaching and encouraged to seek out the full spectrum of identities over the course of their classroom practicum experience.

The Impact of the Application of This Touchstone/Tool

Using the Social Identity Prism as a year-long frame had a clear impact not only on the way student teacher cohorts were able to move beyond the narrow categories of personhood and build more authentic relationships as a group, but it had a tremendous impact on students in their classrooms. From kindergartners studying dance in a unit developed by a student teacher to middle school students examining Persian poetry while reading *Everything Sad Is Untrue*, students responded positively and openly to nuanced and varied ways of being human.

Tips to Keep in Mind if You're Thinking about Using This Touchstone/Tool

This tool is most powerful if it can be used and reflected upon over time and then truly applied to teaching practice or "ways of being" in a school or group within a school. It's one thing to live on the wall, and it's quite another for it to exist in the realm of experience.

Special Notes about Contacting Me for Consultation

Please feel free to contact me at heatherwoodcock12@gmail.com.

Contribute a Praxis Pointer!

If you'd like to share how you have used a Diversity Without Divisiveness Touchstone or Tool, please use this QR Code to contact Dr. Hoyt.

Notes

1 Fields, B. J., and Fields, K. E. (2012). *Racecraft: The Soul of Inequality in American Life*. Verso.
2 Piper, A. (2018). *Escape to Berlin*. APRA Foundation Berlin.
3 Information on Zvi Bekerman can be found at: Center for Comparative Conflict Studies (CFCCS), info@cfccs.org